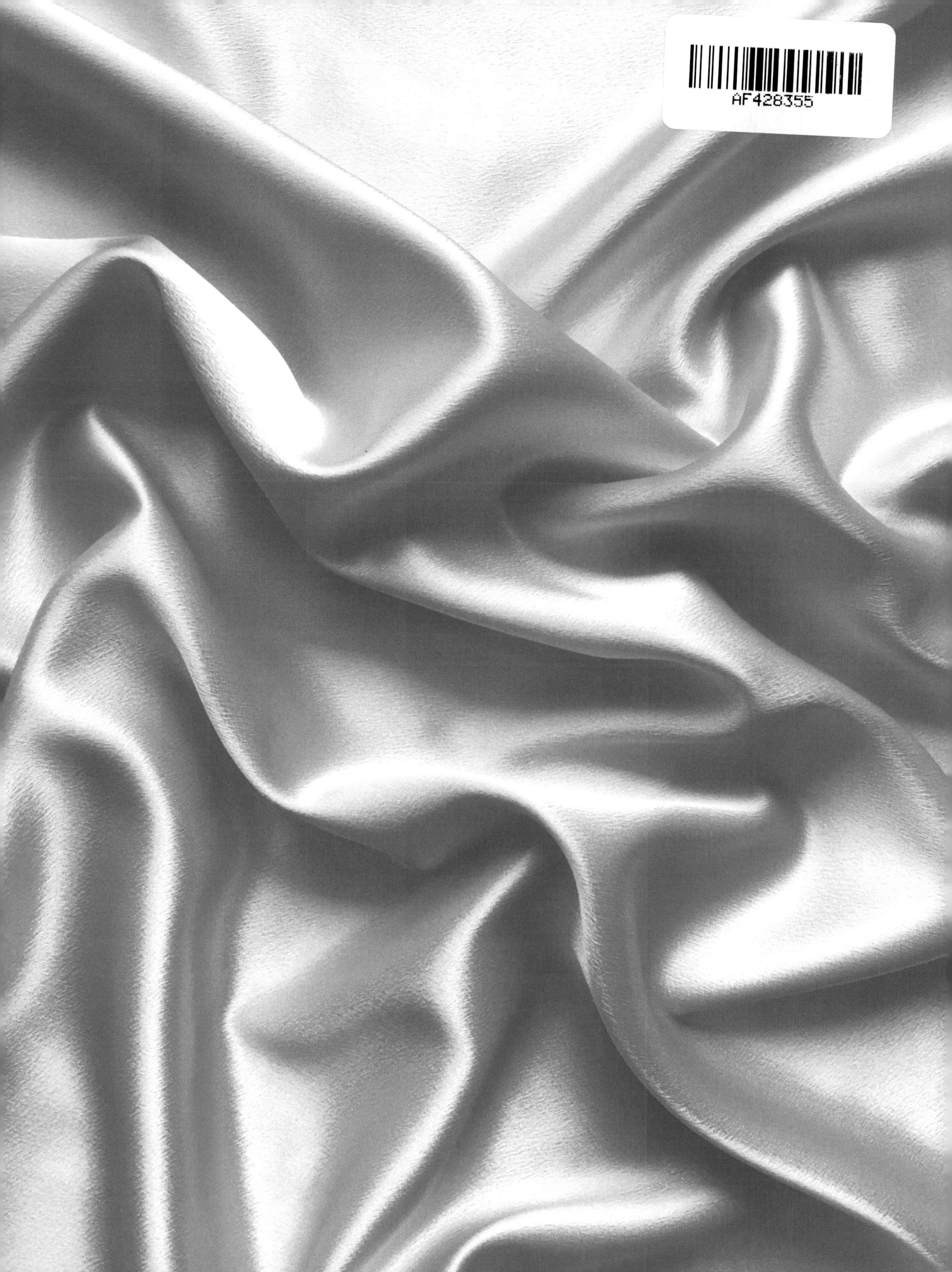
AF428355

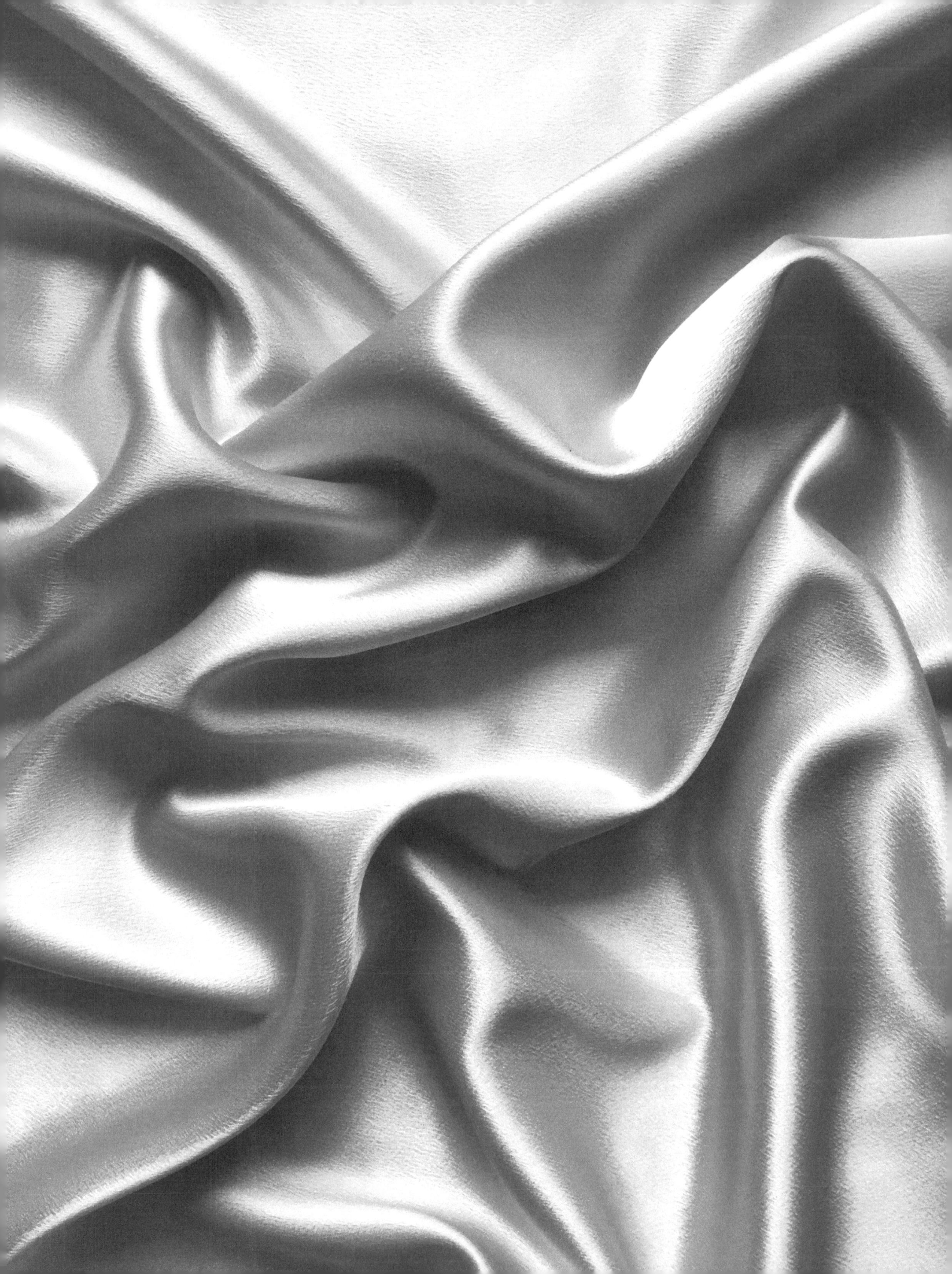

THE WOMAN WITHIN
Memory as Muse

Tami Phelps & Kerry Dean Feldman
with Richard J. Murphy

Published by

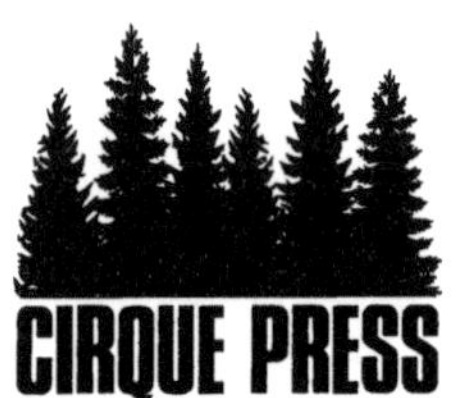

Sandra Kleven — Michael Burwell
3157 Bettles Bay Loop
Anchorage, AK 99515

cirquejournal@gmail.com
www.cirquejournal.com

Cover art: Tami Phelps, "Meet Willow"
Artist photo, Tami Phelps
Book design by Carleen Dawn Photography & Design

Print ISBN: 979-8-88992-071-7

To Tami,
Poetry should be like the one piece of candy the little girl who grew up in a sod house in North Dakota got at Christmas time. She would hold it, smell it, hide it away, take it out again, taste it and somehow make it last for a long time. Enjoy poetry one little taste at a time.

Mrs. Shaw

A Little Treasury of American Poetry, edited by Oscar Williams, 1948, was given as a graduation gift in 1976 to Tami Phelps from Mrs. Vicki Shaw, her gymnastics coach. Tami was the captain of the West Anchorage High School girl's gymnastics team. Mrs. Shaw wrote this inscription in the book that Tami cherishes.

Other books by Tami Phelps and Kerry Dean Feldman

Tami Phelps
Miss Tami, Is Today Tomorrow? Kindergarten in Alaska: Stories for Grown-Ups. Illustrated by Tammy Murray. With Kerry Dean Feldman. Circles, an imprint of Cirque Press, 2021.

Kerry Dean Feldman
Alice's Trading Post: A Novel of the West. Five Star/Gale, 2022, and Thorndike Press, large print edition, 2022.
Kettle Dance: Murder in the Big Sky. Cirque Press, 2022.
Drunk on Love: Twelve Stories to Savor Responsibly. Cirque Press, 2019.

Table of Contents

To the child within us all,
and the stories this child might offer to share with others,
and possibly even with ourselves.

Tami Phelps

Preface

I have heard advice given to writers to "write what you know." I have taken that advice to heart with my artwork. My art is about what I know. Over the last ten years I have made artwork in a variety of mediums in various forms, primarily about women as is reflected in the four sections of this book, *The Woman Within: Memory as Muse*.

So, how did my art about women end up in a book? The short answer is COVID–19. I was elated to have been invited shortly before the pandemic by K N Goodrich of Cyrano's Art Gallery in Anchorage to have a solo exhibit. At that time, I had only a handful of my vintage dress paintings completed that had caught her eye on my Facebook posts. I felt validated as an artist and inspired, then COVID hit. The gallery had to cancel my exhibit as happened to many artists around the world. I was devastated. I lost my creative spark and was in a funk. It was then that my writer-husband, Kerry Dean Feldman, suggested we write a book together about my artwork paired with his poems. That gave me a purpose. My studio became my COVID happy place. Fourteen paintings, fourteen poems, and many months later we were invited by Sandra Kleven and Michael Burwell of Cirque Press to publish a book about *The Woman Within* after they saw the art and read the poetry. Sandra viewed the original paintings hanging on our home walls.

Shortly after this I was invited by Georgia Blue of Georgia Blue Gallery to exhibit some of my earlier art at Snow City Café in downtown Anchorage, which President Barack Obama visited during his trip to Alaska. I showed Georgia a few of my "Woman Within" paintings in hopes that they would work for what she was looking for at the café. They didn't. Instead, she became animated and excited, wanting to exhibit my collection at her gallery. I told her about the possibility of pairing my paintings with Kerry's poetry in a book. She was familiar with my artwork and Kerry's writing and suggested that the intimacy of our work and stories would exhibit better in a gallery setting. On the spot, she scheduled the launch of *The Woman Within* book and exhibition for April 2023 at Georgia Blue Gallery.

The Woman Within book has four sections: I. "The Woman Within," II. "Her Stories," III. "Growing Panes: Reflections on an Amaryllis," and finally, IV. "Pleased To Meet You."

The book is co-written by Tami Phelps and Kerry Dean Feldman, with photographer Richard J. Murphy who graciously agreed to include his phenomenal photographic art in the Amaryllis section.

It is my hope that you will find this book a thing of beauty and a joy forever. That you will enjoy it "a taste at a time" and might also reflect on your own stories within.

- Tami Phelps

I

THE WOMAN WITHIN

Art and Photographs by Tami Phelps
Poems by Kerry Dean Feldman

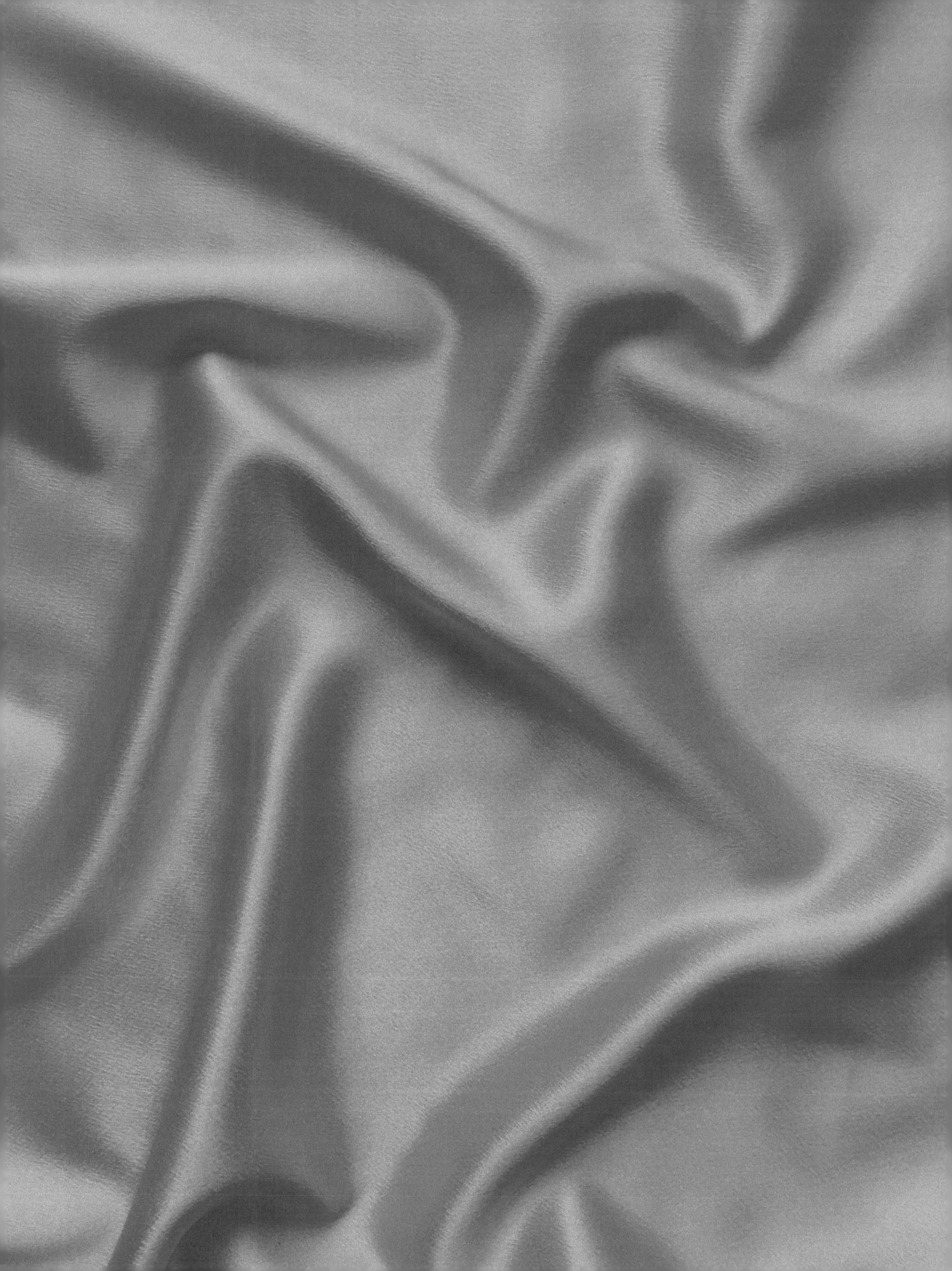

Introduction

I wanted to tell a story about the child within a woman, about her memories of girlhood, because every time I go to an antique store, I imagine the lives lived with those things that are now called antiques. (Funny how more and more I see items from my era and life in antique stores.) I bought a vintage white baby dress that I adhered on wood cradleboard and "camouflaged" with a cold wax painting so that the dress was almost invisible against clouds in the sky, like a memory. But the dress was still seen there.

I painted "Meet Willow" first. When I started this project, I referred to the works as "a child within." But this seemed limiting. There's history in a vintage dress, and I wanted a dress to be a representation of a life lived, a historical measurement of time, not a child within a dress, but a woman within each dress. A woman with stories to tell.

I wanted more about the universal aspects of being a woman than the personal focus of my prior two exhibitions about "being female." A few of these works here relate to my own experiences, like the butterflies, a girl's first period, and "Expectations." Most bring in elements of the natural world, not the personal female cultural worlds of my prior exhibitions.

When Kerry began to write from a man's perspective about the woman within a girl, as he saw me work on each, I was impressed by the element of respect in his writing. He put into words aspects of what I wanted to convey with my art work. These were not just "cute little girl dresses art." They are intended to create awareness of the respect due young girls from any cultural background.

These vintage dresses are canvases on which I tell my stories.

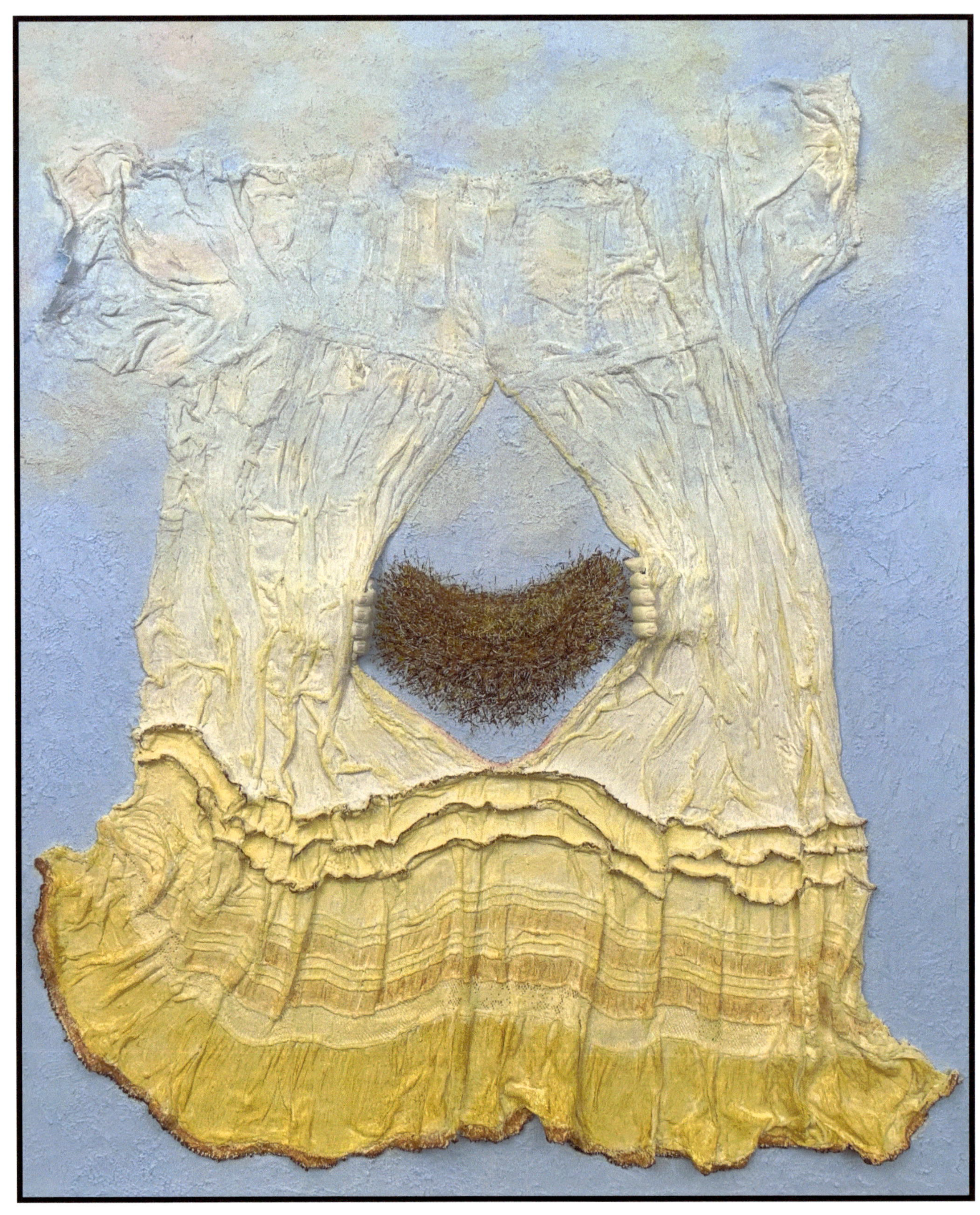

EXPECTATIONS

EXPECTATIONS

Holding my daughter,
she wails her demand to be fed,
the only sound she seems
to know after a few spins
around the sun.
I say, "If I had breasts
I could feed you," and imagine
orbs on my chest that she sucks,
and finds food. Felt good,
but strange, like a sci-fi movie
which, actually, they are–these bodies
we inhabit but do not invent.

As if we are stories
waiting to be told
by the anatomy into which we slip
like comfortable, peculiar, gloves.

Wombs become thoughts,
become wishes,
become babies.

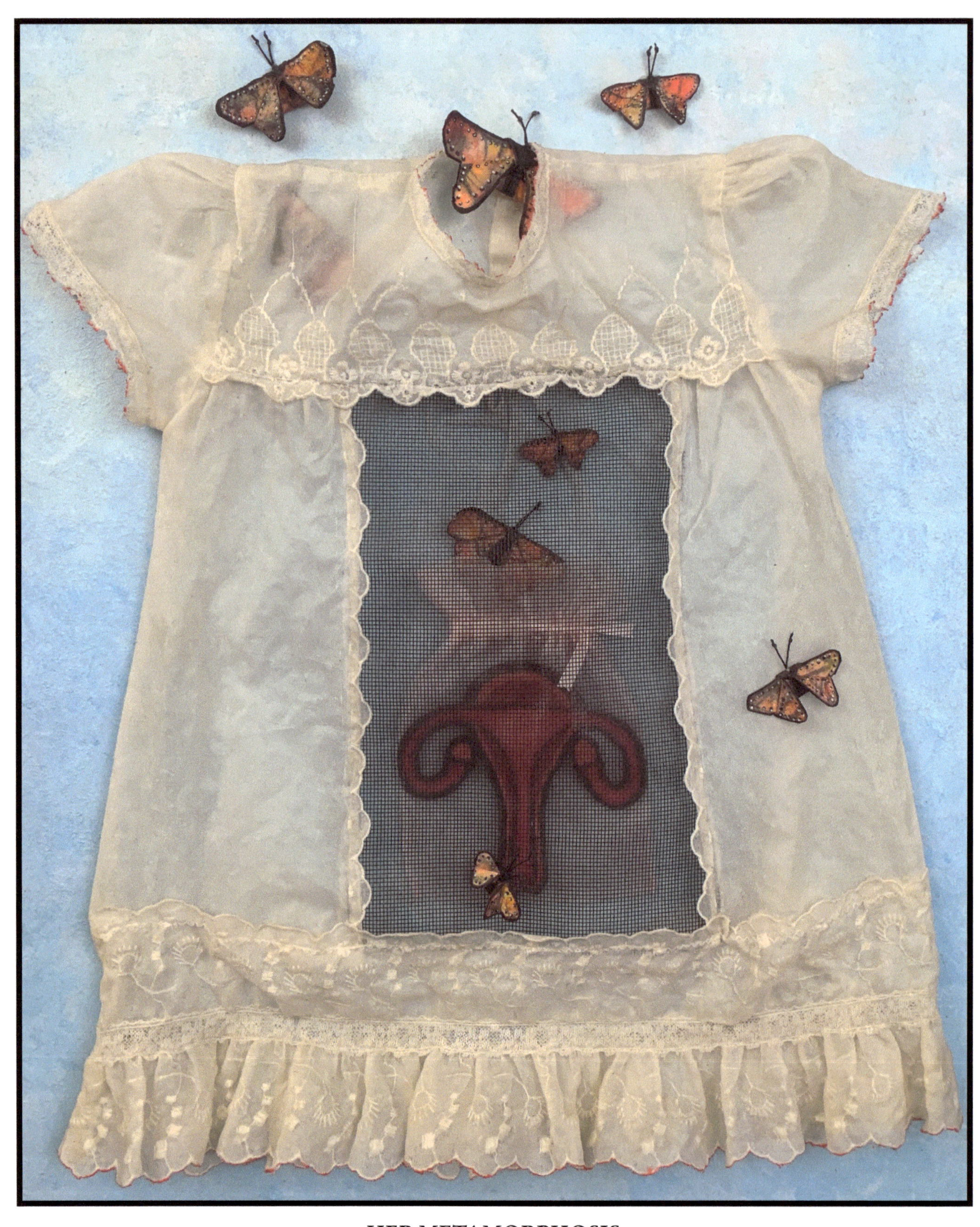

HER METAMORPHOSIS

WHAT DO YOU SAY?

What do you say
to your daughter's daughter
the first time you see her
in their bungalow home,
asking a dog to move aside
from center stage.

How do they

make a harbor for life
inside their bodies,
just as they received,
just as this bundled baby
might someday do.

And, oh, the delight
to play hide and seek
when she's four,
her delight in fooling me,
like her mom when she was young.
Helping her grow up,
feel Grampa love,
and presents—an Elsa dress,
caterpillars to nurture to winged miracles.
Her announcing, "I'm a mother, now, too."
Age three. She feeds her babies
leaves, then sugar power
in oranges for flight muscles.
One day she announces, "It's time,"

time to set them free
like mothers must do,
and fathers, though we cry
inside.

She opens the butterfly cage.
Sunny day, it's time.
One by one, wings flutter,
find the opening, flee
to the unknown.
But one clings to home.
Afraid? And I wonder
if my daughter feared flying, too.
"You can do it,"
my granddaughter says
to her reluctant child, "fly!"

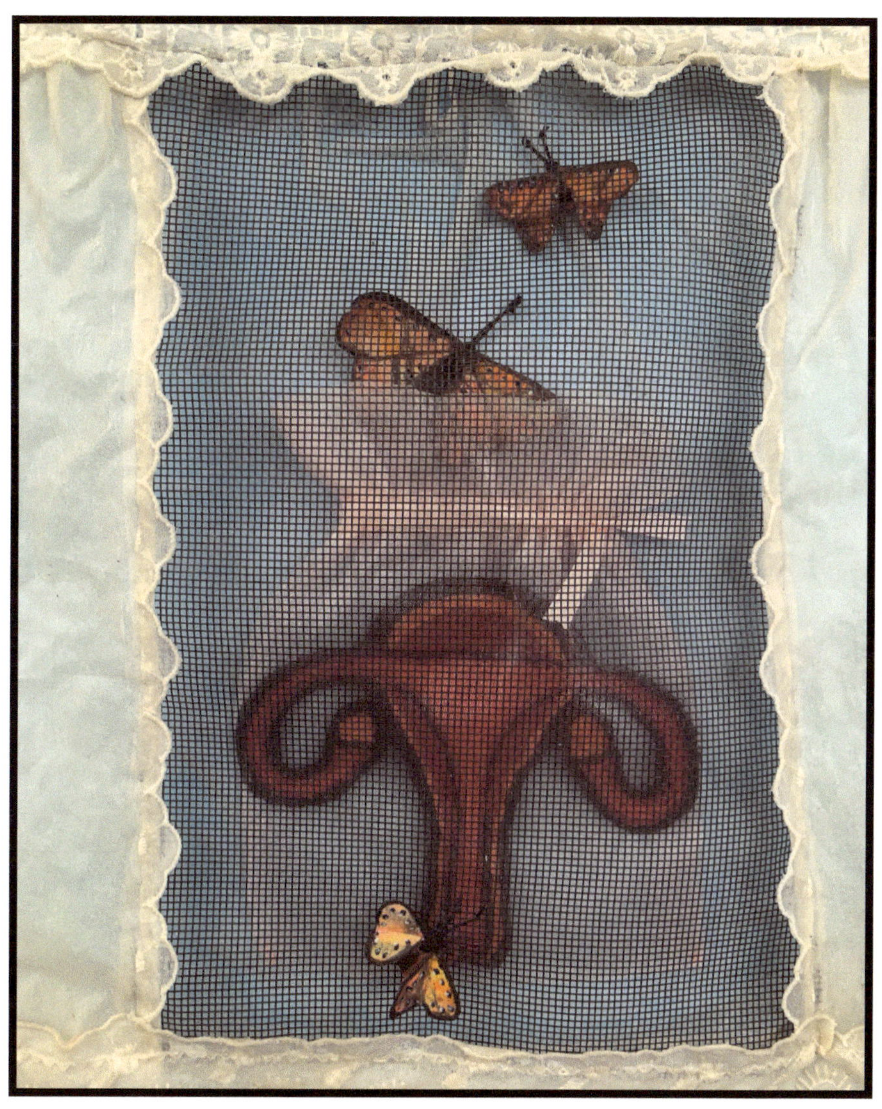

HER METAMORPHOSIS (detail)

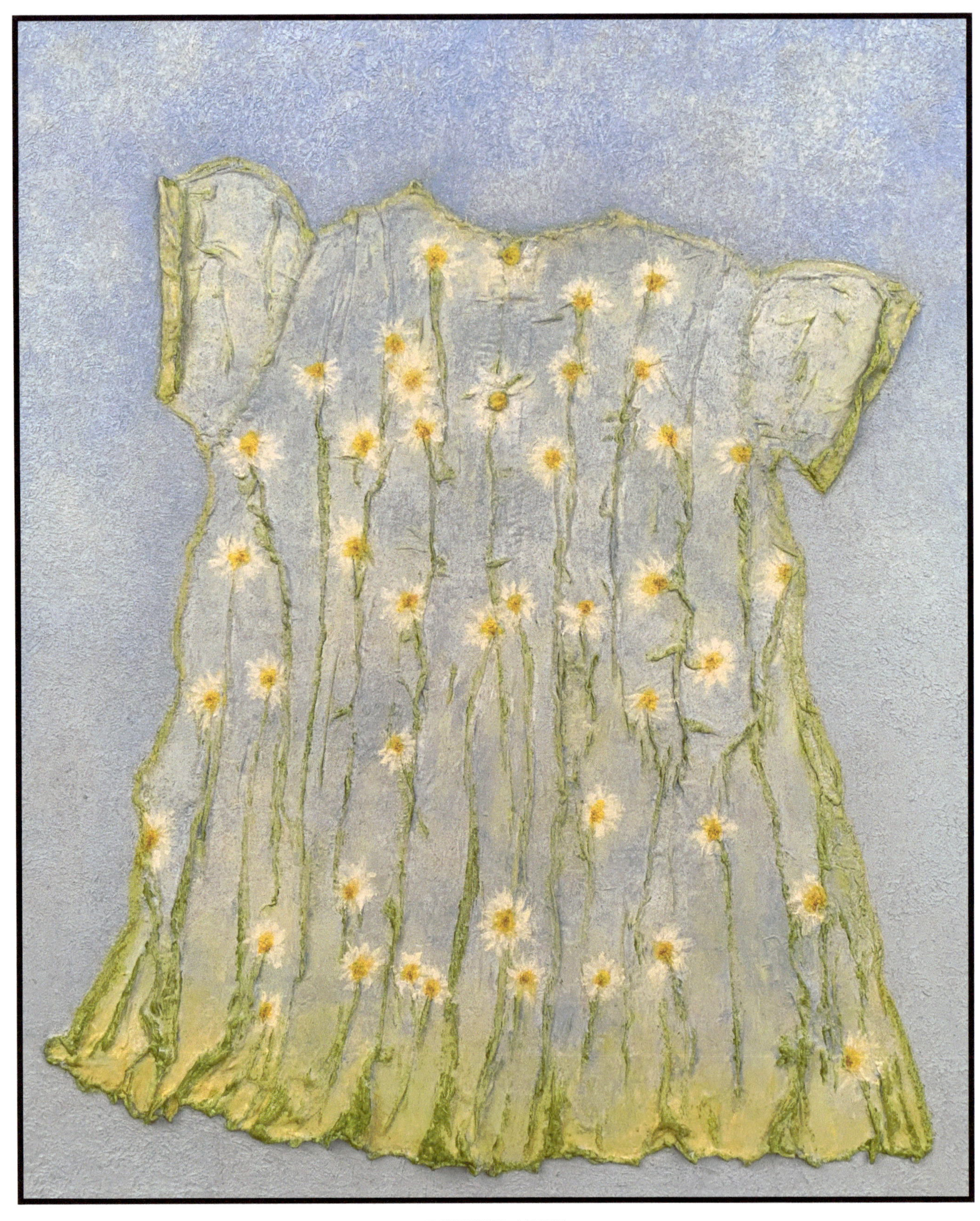

MEET DAISY

DO YOU REMEMBER WHEN?

Do you remember when they held you
after storms? So many over the years,
never asking for thanks.
No matter you deserved your wreck,
no matter the fault,
always their arms, hearts open to you,
— the most lovely bay man knows
after a rough sail.

Are you glad you changed their diapers?

Glad you let her bike ram you
that day on a road instead of
riding to her death on a busy street?

Glad you let the other curl fingers
in your hair as you sang her to sleep?
Glad you drove her to the western shore,
to her new life, her kids to follow.
All now grown as she
sings grandkids to sleep,
tiny fingers curl in her hair.

Words from each arrive each spring
as surely as an Equinox,
no matter your innocence, wealth,
or fame: "Happy Birthday, dear Brother.
I love you."

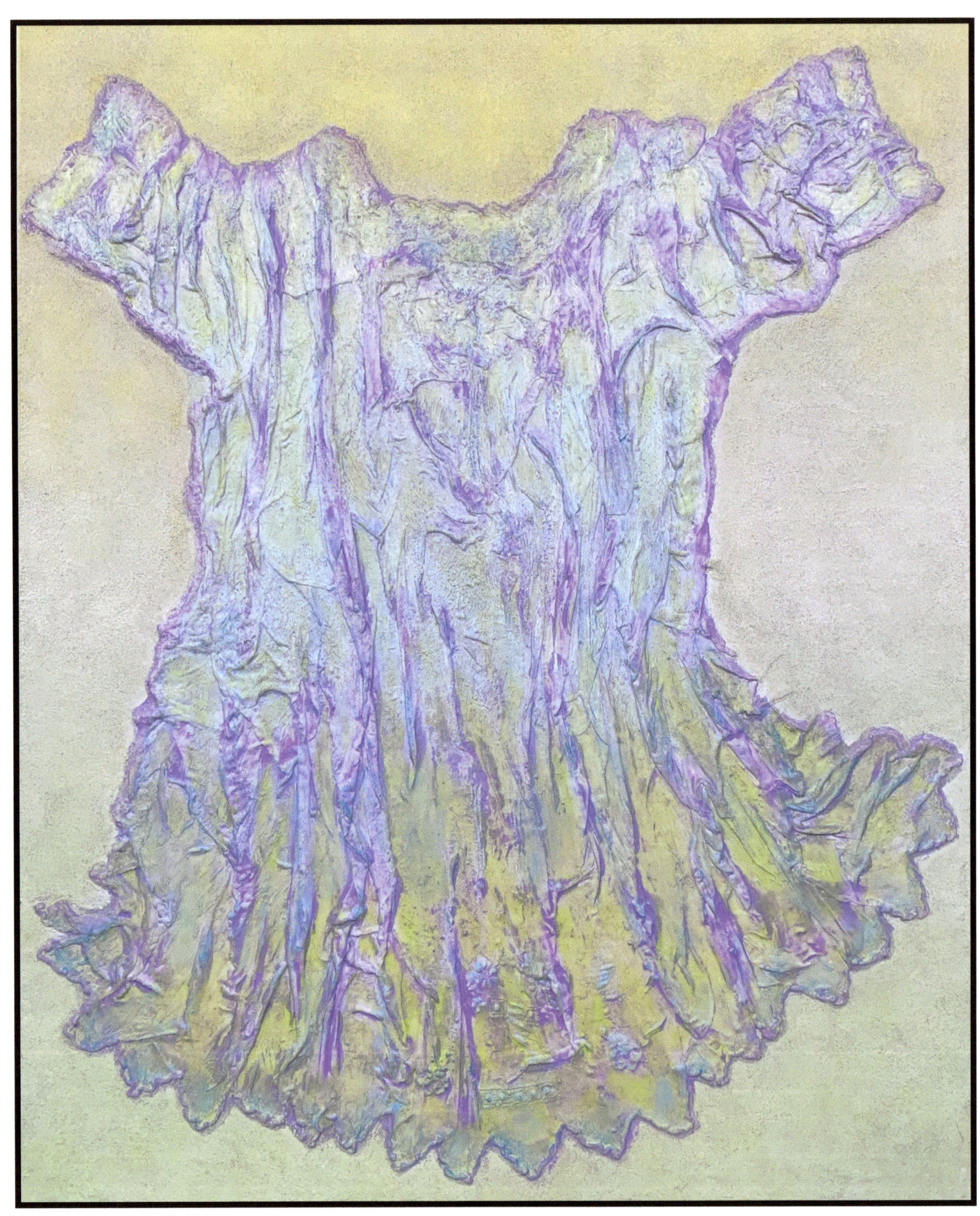

MEET AURORA

RIDING ASTEROIDS

There was nothing, short of riding asteroids,
to flutter a boy's unsuspecting heart,
like a girl with pompoms jumping high
in a gym, curls akimbo, short skirt flying
above her bony knees;
nothing, he silently admits, amazed
that an ordinary day could hold such
mystery, certainly not his, until now.

Yet, there she giggles, oblivious
of his discovery of the meaning
of life. Her not needing to know
him, yet, nor his admiration of her,
to fulfill her pompom destiny.

Today, that boy might chant,
"Ride, Sally, Ride!" as she
zooms past rocks, weightless,
fulfilling a destiny her mom
imagined for her, ensconced
in her spaceship, umbilically
pumped full of life and possibility.

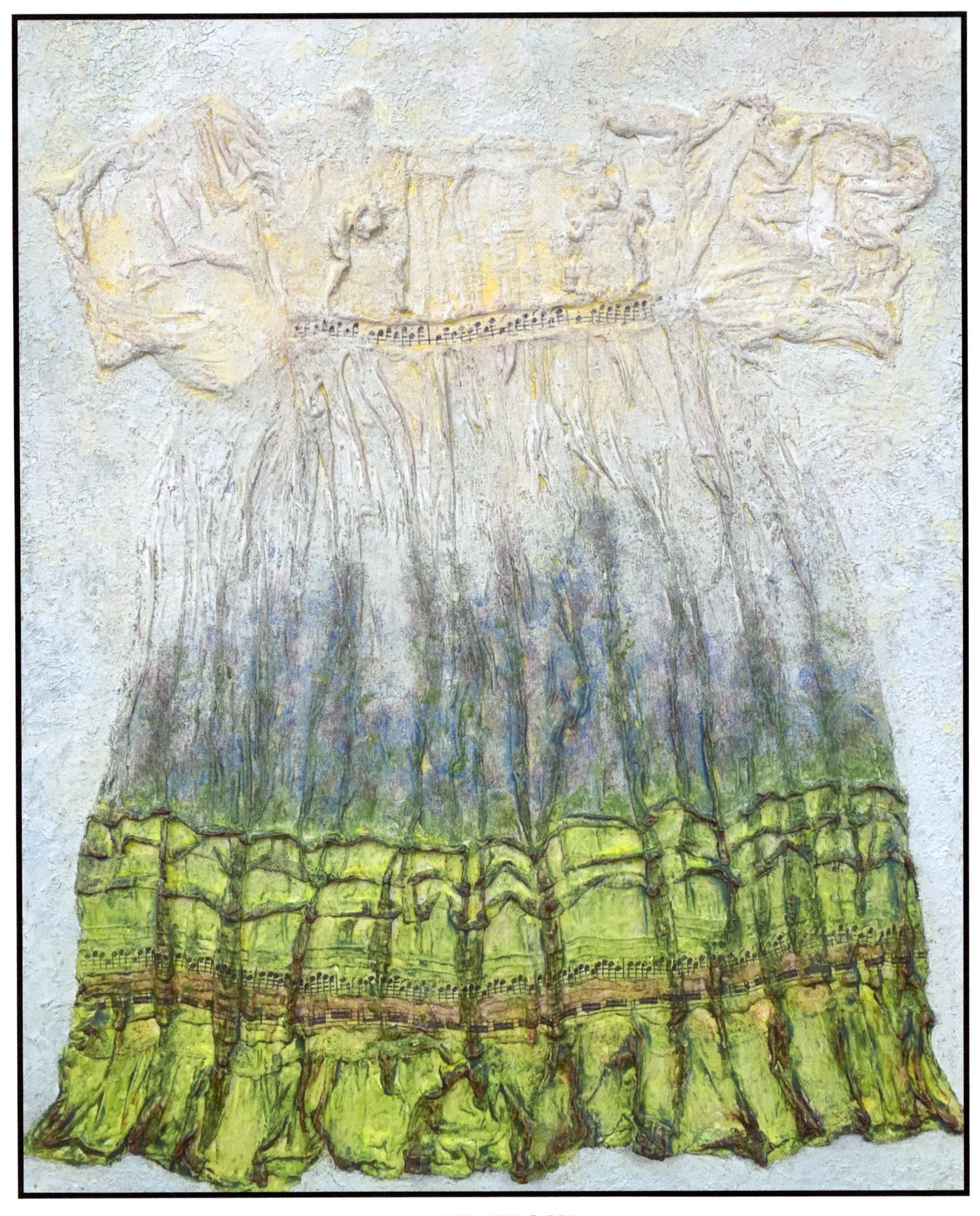

MEET MELODY

SAFE

Two days old, she tries
to see me from the sterile room.
Safe now, after the perilous ride
in a womb—a room
none of us recalls.

Safe, safe now, thank God,
she is safe at last, out here,
where

she learns to walk, talk,
read like other kids; run,
compete, excel. Later cook,
ride a bike, clean her room,
dance to music. Graduate.

I watch from a distance
over the years. She achieves
prominence, the American dream.

"Keep your hands on the wheel
when cops pull you over!"
her mother tells her,
remembering Breonna,
and so many girls like her.
Words I never had to tell my daughter,
though they played together as girls.

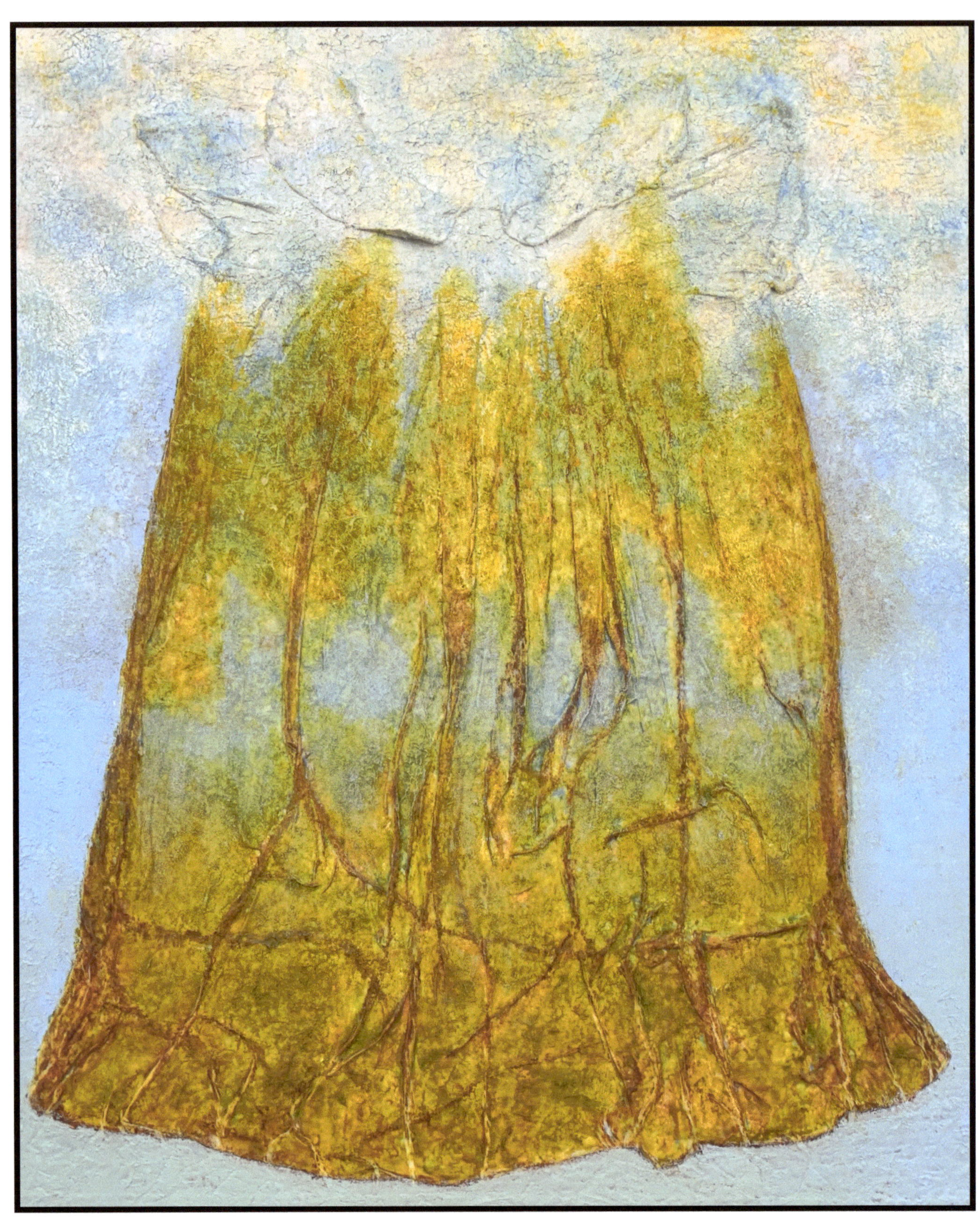

MEET WILLOW

PIRATES
 (for Koleen)

We climbed northern trees, my sister
and I, hid like pirates from passers-by.
She seemed happy to pursue my games,
a slender vine becoming woman
someday, far from pirating.
Not me. I discovered my world
evolved into a world men made,
stepping only into larger jeans.
Her path had forks along the way.
No hints, never suspected,
in our pirate tree.

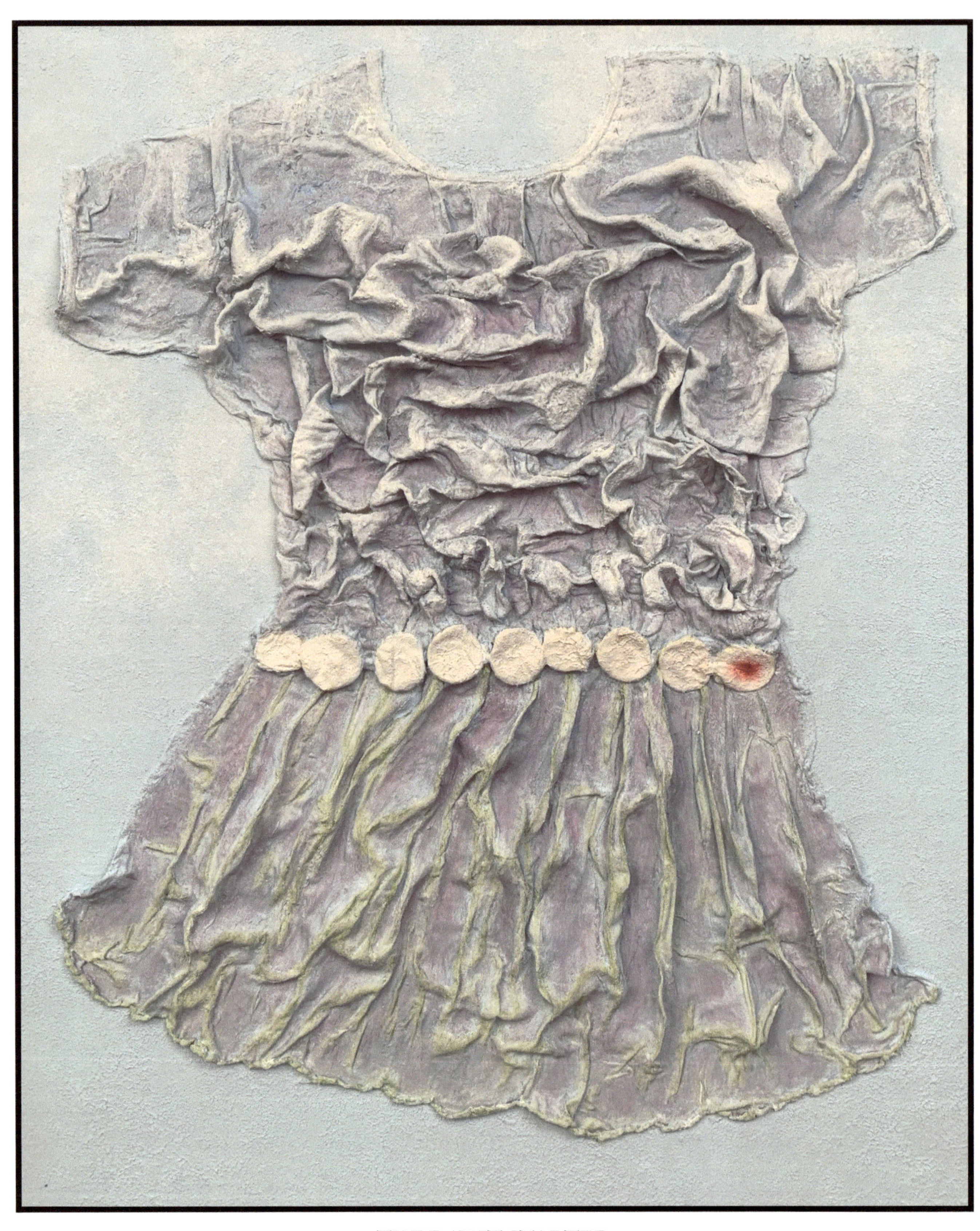

THE DAY IT STARTED

THE DAY IT STARTED

I.
Dad! she cries, hurting,
running to the bathroom.
 I follow.
"Yes?"
It hurts, hurts ... I need ...
I drive fast to the 7-11.
A sari-clad woman greets me,
a red dot between her eyes.
She stares at the winged package
on the counter, smiles.
I gaze at her red dot.

II.
I was prepared for that day
decades before, by a sister
bent over in pain by a hurt
I'd never know.
A mystery beyond baseball, wrestling,
pirates, fishing with flies or Superman capes.
Unlike most mysteries—*Supernova* or
Black Hole—this held the mystery of human life
including me, but I never heard a Sonata
in its honor.

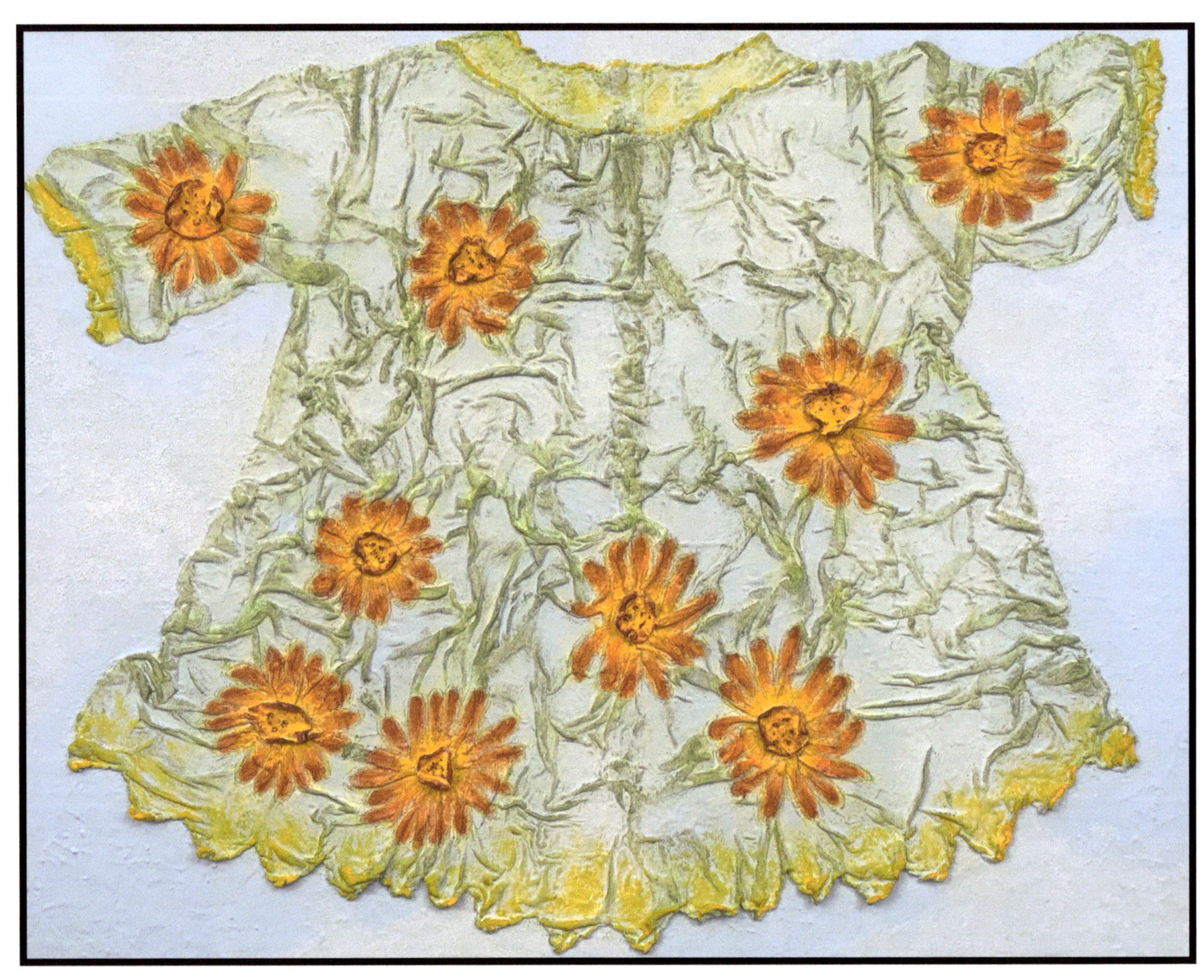

MEET ZINNIA

CAMPED AT ELEPHANT POINT

Farther north than I thought I'd ever be,
a gang of girls peeks in,
laughing in chilled salty air
at my research stuff—
a scale to weigh muktuk,
cameras, pens, sleeping bag
and canned food for a month.
Their ancestors breathed here
thousands of years before my nylon tent,
laughing together at odd sights in a day,
long ago, like these young women
preparing to take their place.

Decades later, their joy tears into me
when I learn of another corpse,
abandoned like an empty tin can,
an assailant's seed in her, rotting
along with the beauty in which
she walked, ran, and slept.
Her grieving family, her friends,
reminded they look like her,
the dead woman, girl, could be
any one of them. We should scream
each day in this far north killing field,
until it becomes safe to be a Native girl.

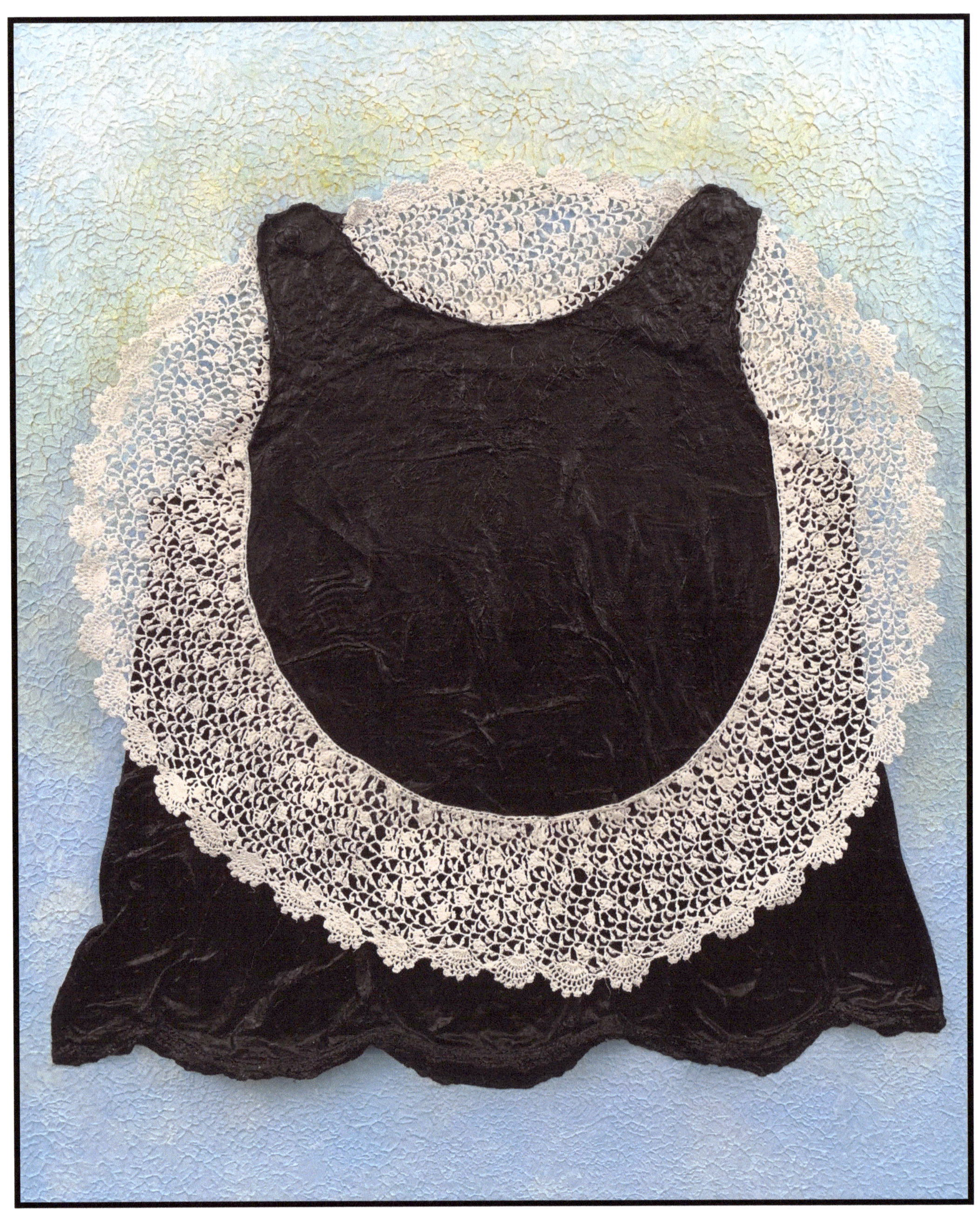

MEET RBG

LOVE (A Haiku)

"Who wrote, *I love K*
in chalk on the bricks, recess?"
(He hoped it was *HER*.)

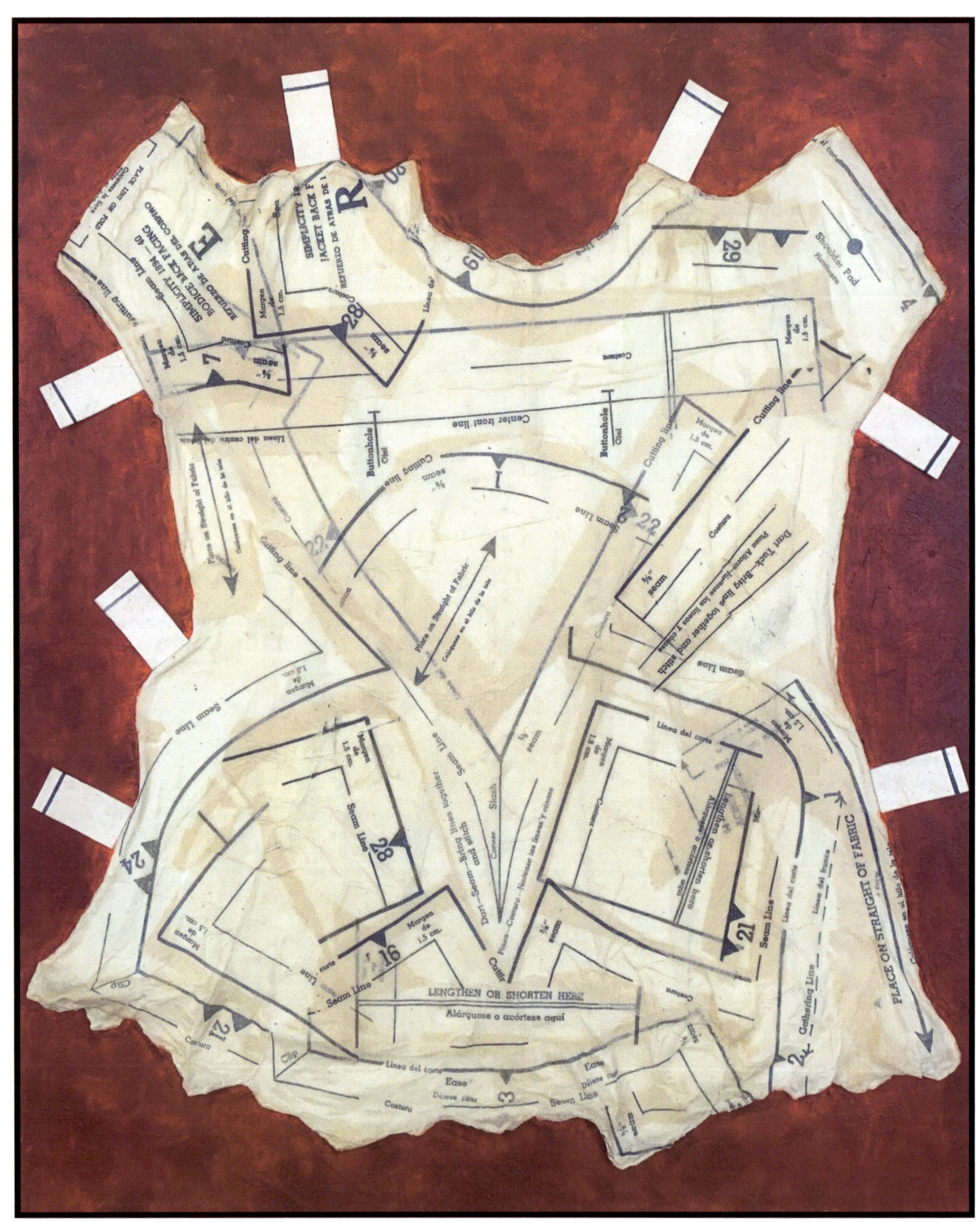

ONE SIZE DOES NOT FIT ALL

ADAM'S RIBS

A hand raised to dispute the prof's lecture.

When do realizations come,
after being born,
that words can fail?
How many twirls around the sun?
Different truth blossoms
in young bodies,
unable to be ignored.

"Male and female," the prof had said,
reflecting the story in Genesis.

"I'm both," the student blurted.
Short hair parted to the side.
Belted jeans. A young man.

After class, the prof wanted
to apologize. "It's okay.
Gotta run, see my gynecologist."

So, which of Adam's ribs
did the Creator use to make
him/her/them? Or give license
to harm such divinely complex humanity?

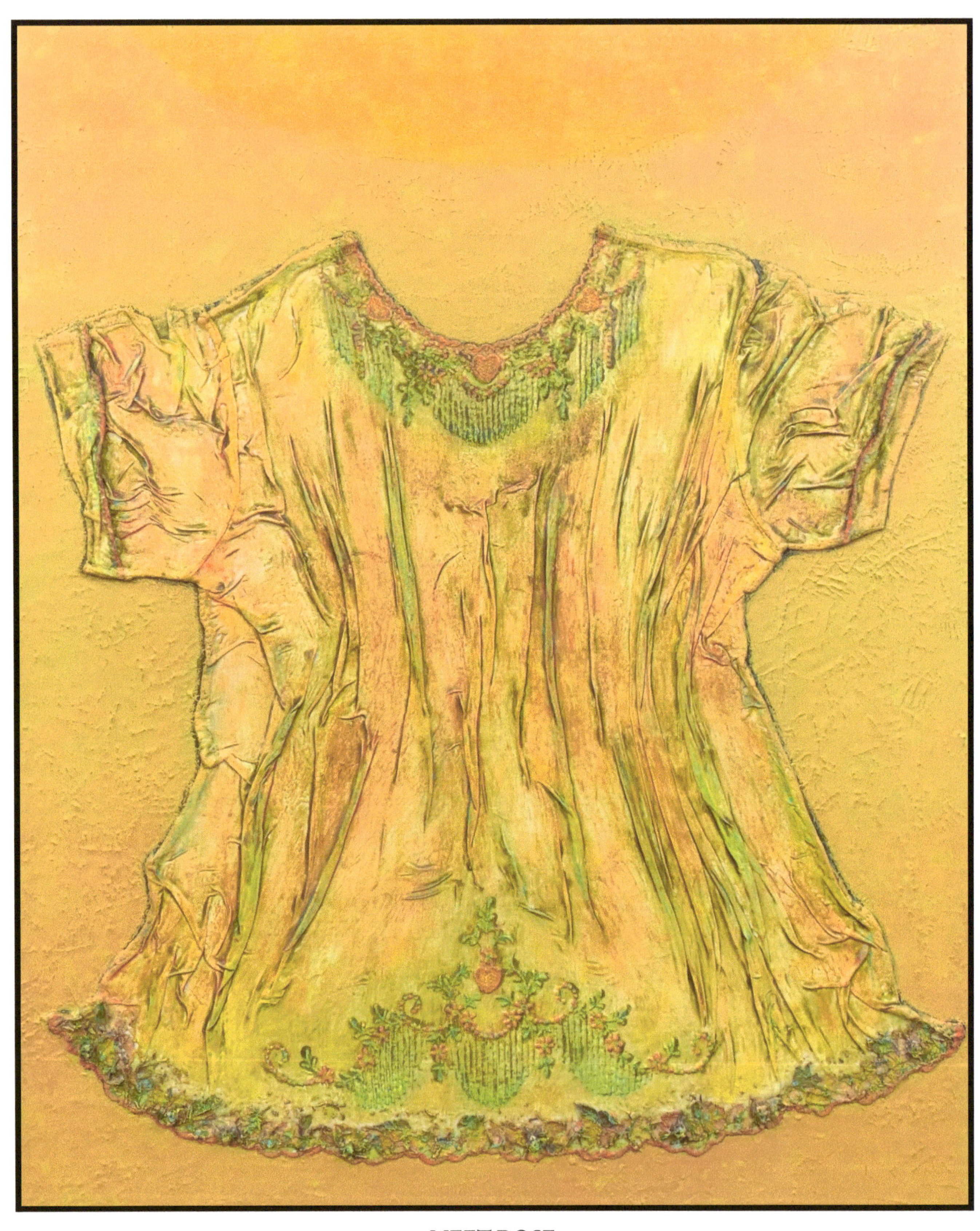

MEET ROSE

LADY, DO YOU KNOW?

Lady, do you know how
I see you?

Not how you see you,
I'm sure. Putting on make-up,
to hide...you.
I see beauty
looking in a mirror
mornings.

I like the curves of you,
perfect, as you lean into beautifying.

Learning that when
so young. Thinking, without paint
you are not beautiful.

I love your fruits as they are.
The full peaches and sweetgrass and eyes.

And you are always innocent
to me. A flower.

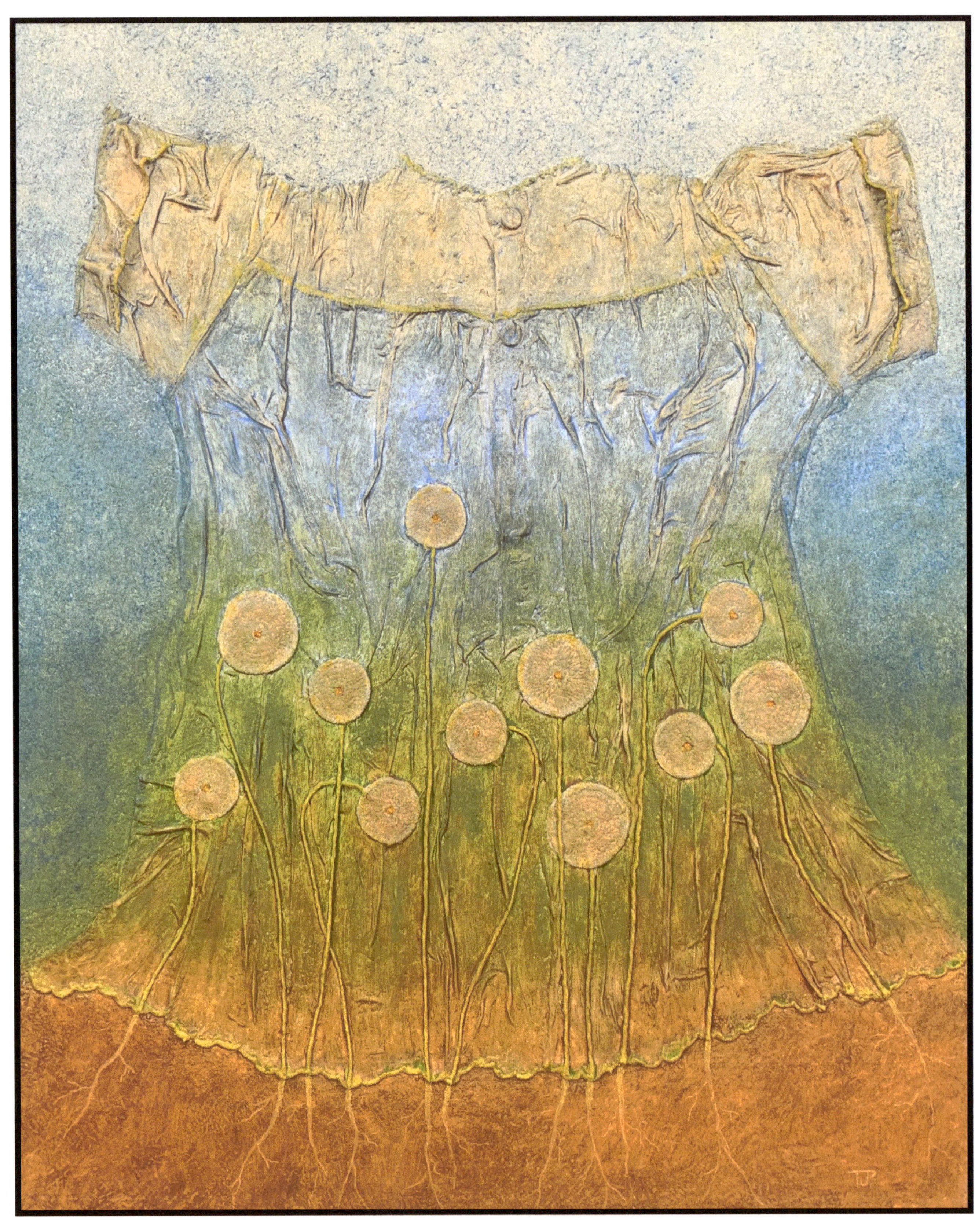

MEET FLORA

MOM

I.
LEARN FROM HORSES, SHE SAID
Once upon a time she was a girl,
that woman there, talking to the horse
in the river, to let her ride him.
Once upon a time that horse was wild.
Before that girl seduced him
with words of trust, almost love.

"You don't break a horse,"
she told me. "You learn from a horse."

What she learned from horses
I can only surmise, but I did what she said.

Here's what I learned from horses:
"Be wild, free, until she talks to you;
words of trust, almost love, discover
what happens."

Was it the bit in my mouth
or the saddle that made me feel safe?
Was it bucking her off?
Or getting her warm wet scrubs
after a day?

Was it being fed,
or the comfort of fences?
Or initials branding me

as hers, enjoying even my seared flesh,
which love must have when it comes?

II.
TUMBLEWEEDS
We were filled with life,
tumbleweeds dancing on dusty roads
in any wind we could find.
Free, though bound to the other
in ways neither understood.

       Our laughter harmonized,
       our anger clashed.

Others came from your body
to whirl and wish with us
that winds would never die;
brothers and sisters drinking cocoa
on wintry days pressed together
in a family album.

Winds took us to other places.
We return to dance and cry in winds
aching around you, around drainpipes
and trees of the house you made a home.

       When tumbleweeds catch a breath against barbed wire,
       clump together like scrawny cattle against corner posts,
       I see my time with you, and all of us, clinging together.

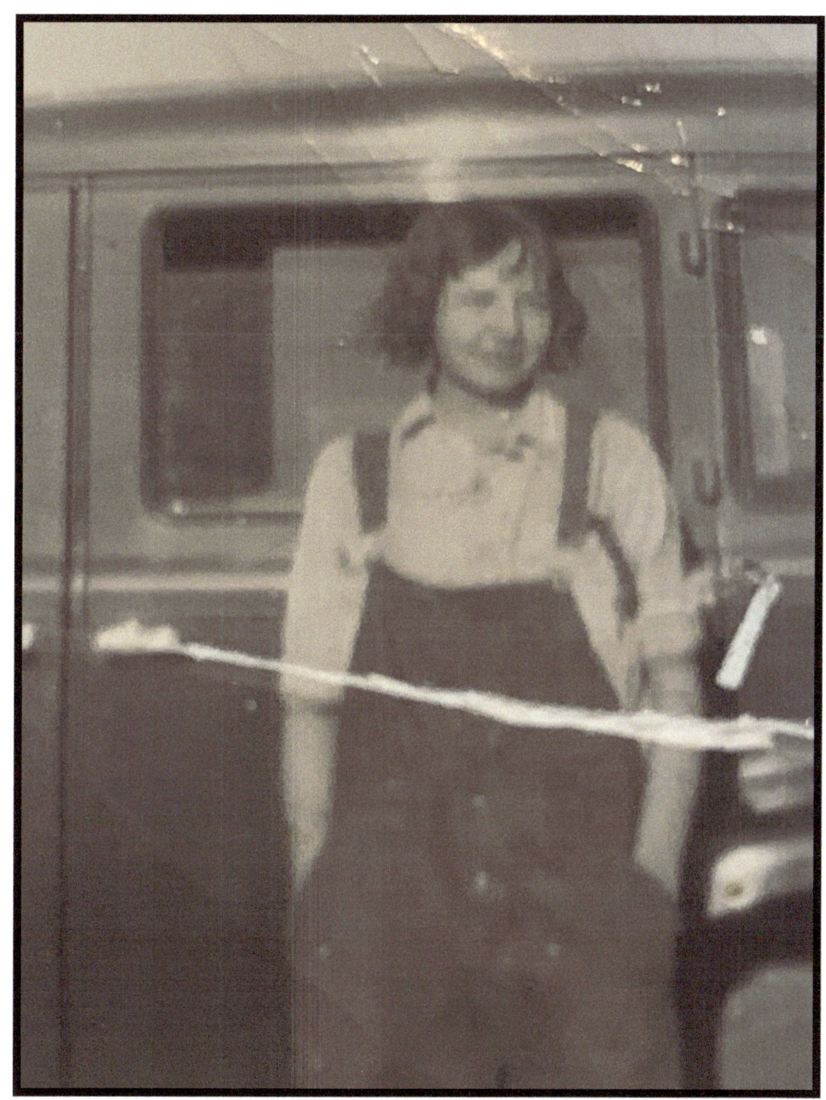

Kerry's mother ("Peaches") in her teens, Montana, ca 1932

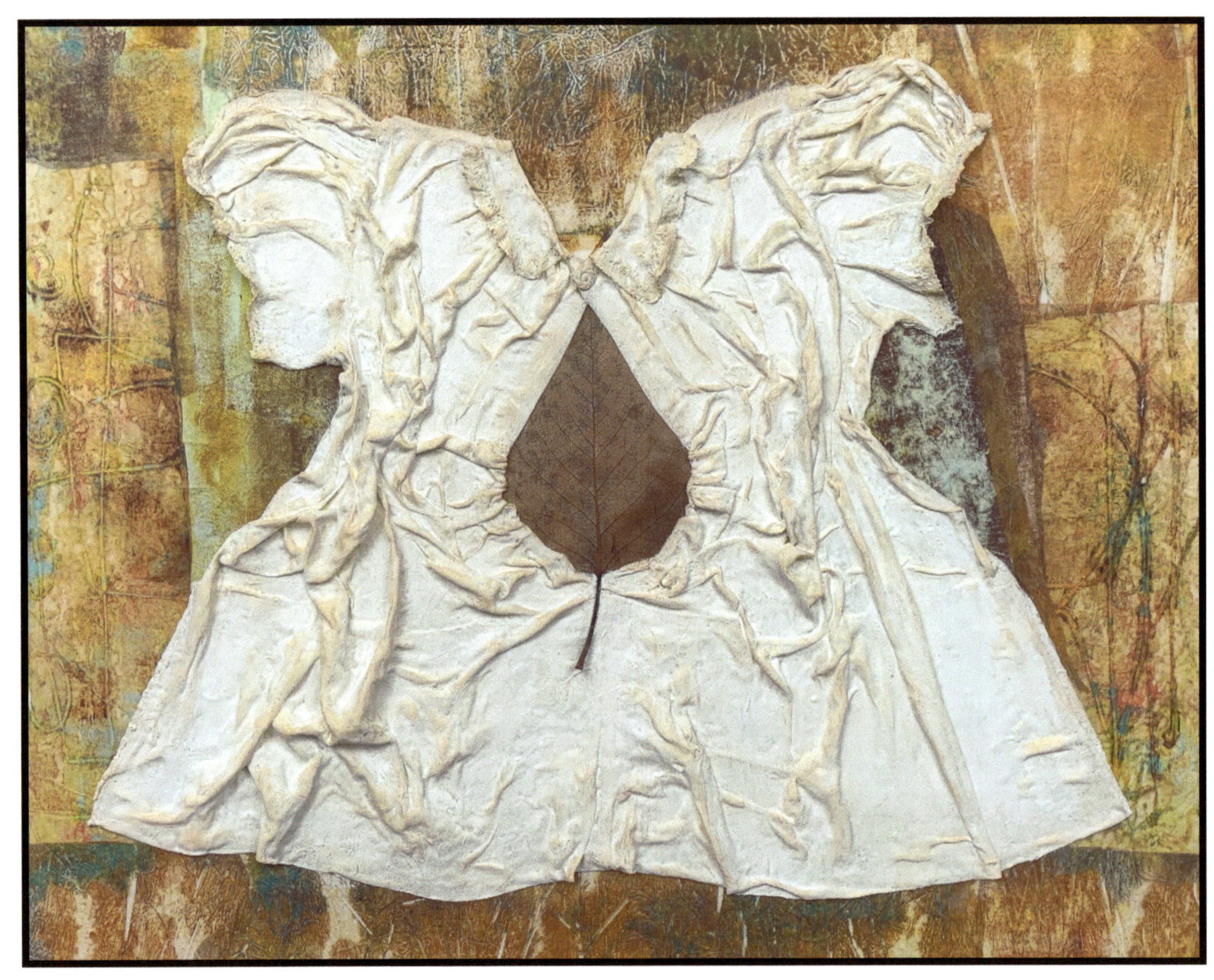

THE AUTUMN OF HER LIFE

RIDING A TRAIN WEST

Dressed in finery,
how a young lady rides a train,
no eye contact with strangers,
how her mother taught her
before she died in childbirth.
Outside, dry land
gobbles her many-lakes greenery,
the weary expanse empty,
sights never seen in her seventeen years.
An occasional hawk surveys
grass for lunch.
Painted cactus, silent sentinels
of survival, of hope.
Lessons from this new land
mock the silk she wears,
more expensive than her father could afford,
but now she's wedded,
off his hands,
into the arms of her suitor,

him traveling westward
in a dung-laden cattle car.
*

 I never saw her history in the pies
she baked for us, the butter
she churned, dabbed on our desserts.

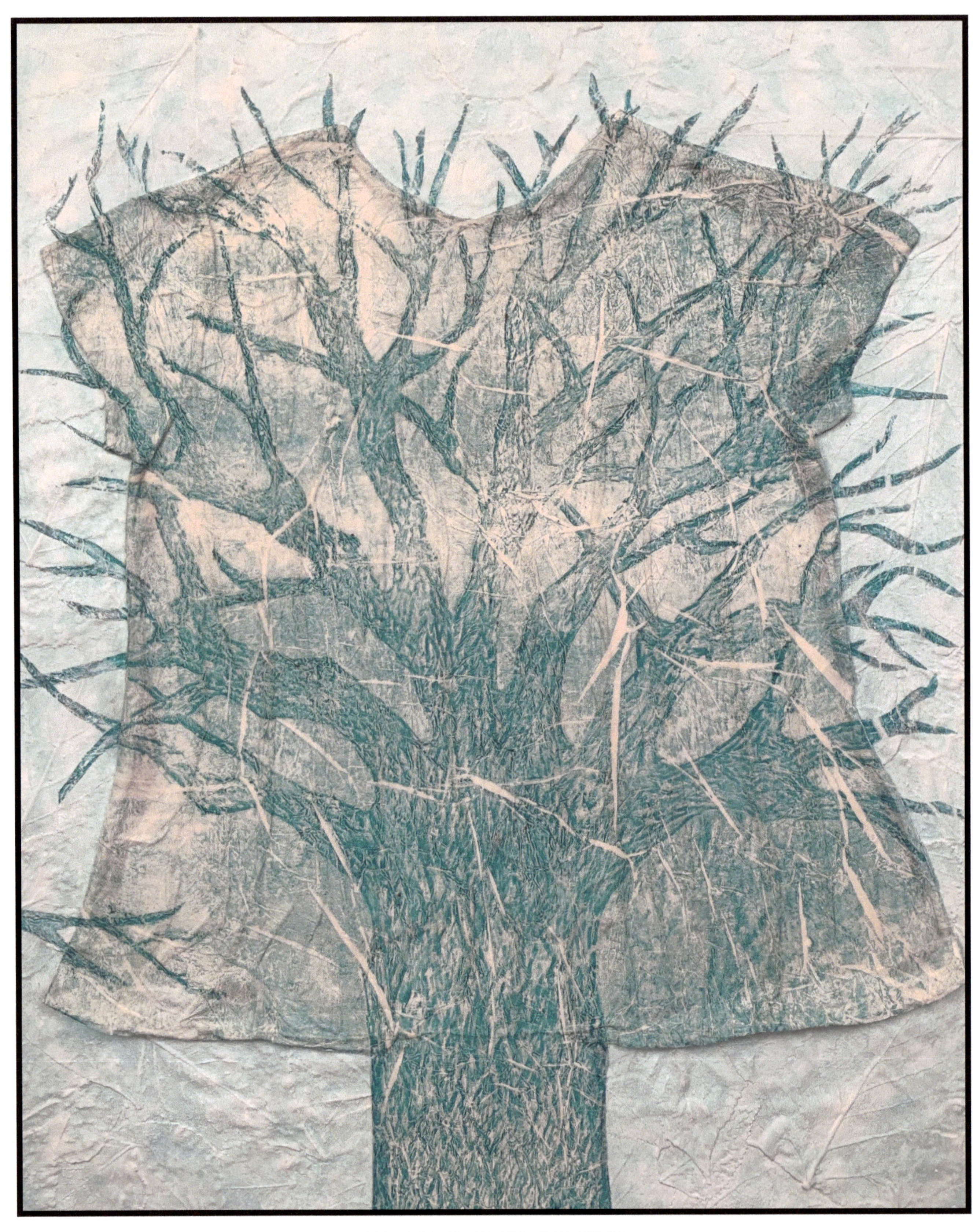

GROUNDED IN WINTER

THE GIRL IS MOTHER OF THE WOMAN

The girl is mother
of the woman, from seed
to glorious stories stored
in limbs, tired legs, and longings.

Who goes to see her now?
Well cared for you hope,
by strangers, women like her
waiting for sod to again
cover them.

Sagging bosom that fed
others, gallant smiles most days.
So quiet now, compared to long ago.

She misses the noise,
needs strung on her
like holiday lights, ornaments
proclaiming need of her,
and so much love.

II

HER STORIES

Art , Photographs, and Text by Tami Phelps

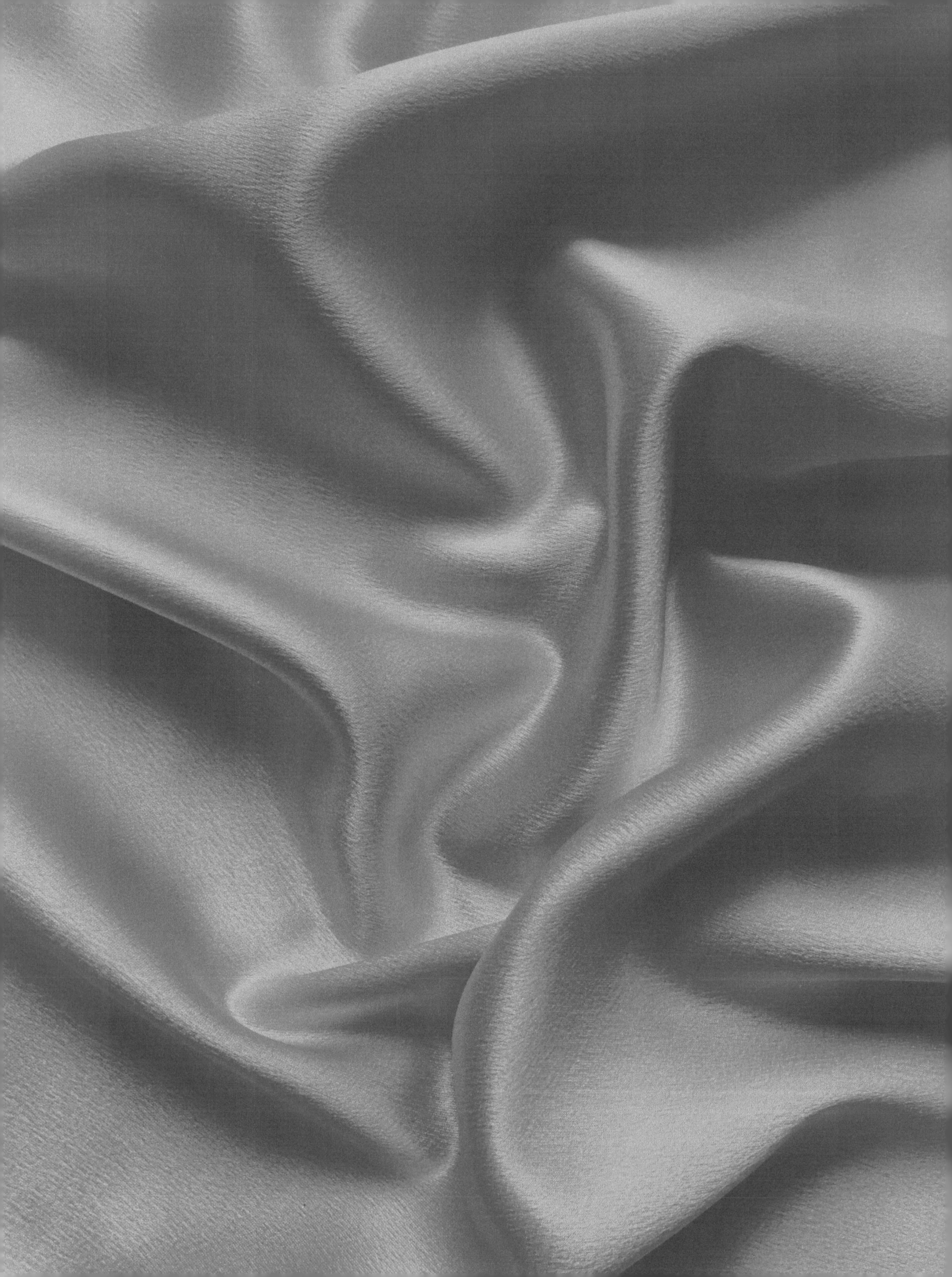

Her Stories

Cold wax and assemblage painting

A day after I first held my granddaughter, her great-grandmother died. Mayla was 42 days old. Her great-grandma, Peaches, just days short of 100 years. The timing of the occasion was emotionally stunning. That was the day my husband and I hung the dress in the tree. That was the day I began to reflect on the meanings of a woman's life, including my own, and start to tell "her stories" through my art. I knew that day affected me. What I didn't know was how deep the feelings went.

Later, I went to a recycled hardware store with two of my brothers in Portland, Oregon where I bought a bucket of rusty metal rods. They told me that the rods are used in construction to hold forms when pouring concrete walls. I use them as "scrolls" attached to my paintings.

They are a way for me to unroll bits of "she-ness" in my artwork. A way to honor the art and the stories I have written inspired by the vintage dress we hung and photographed in the tree on a cold January day in Longmont, Colorado, 2017.

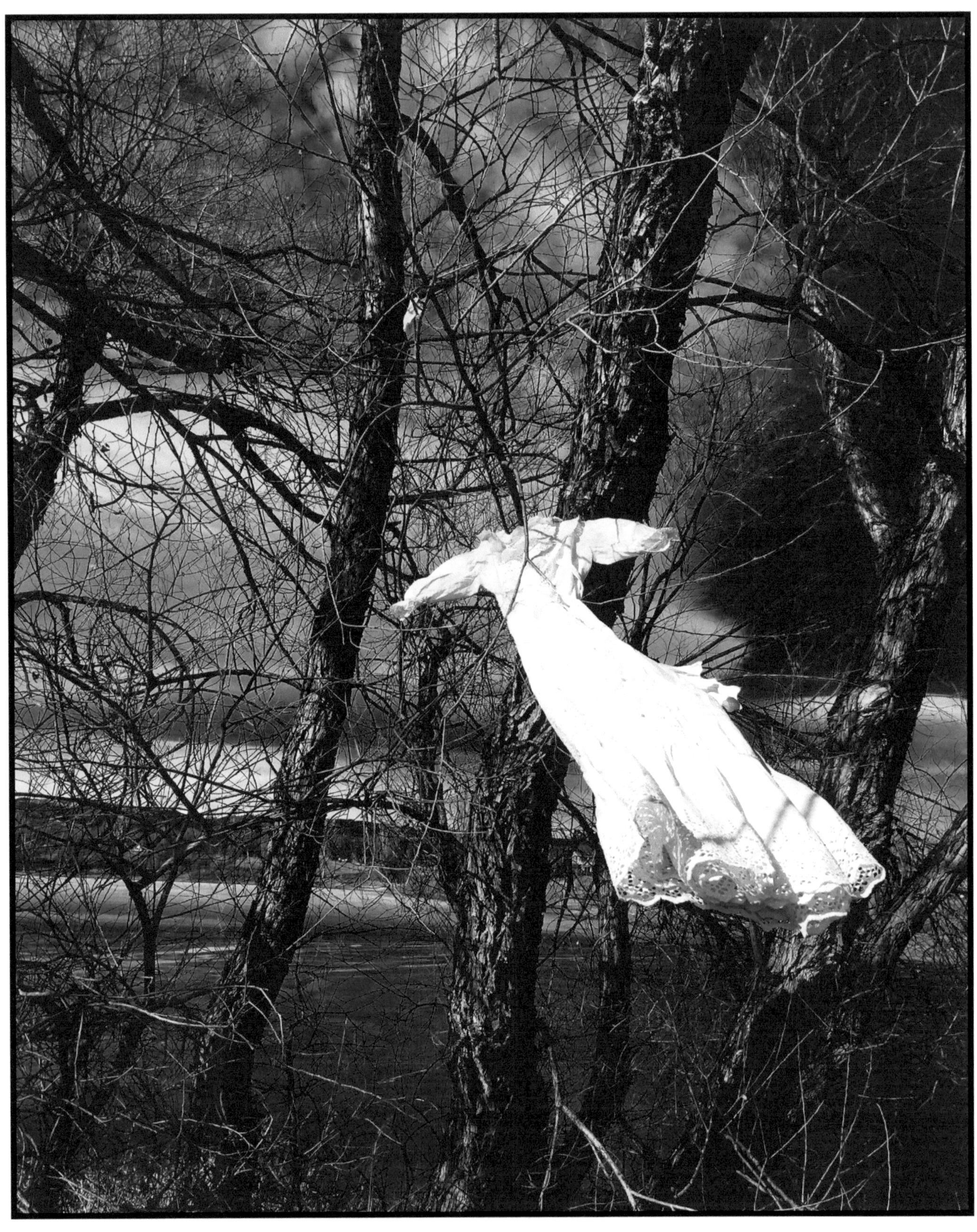

January 2017, Longmont, Colorado

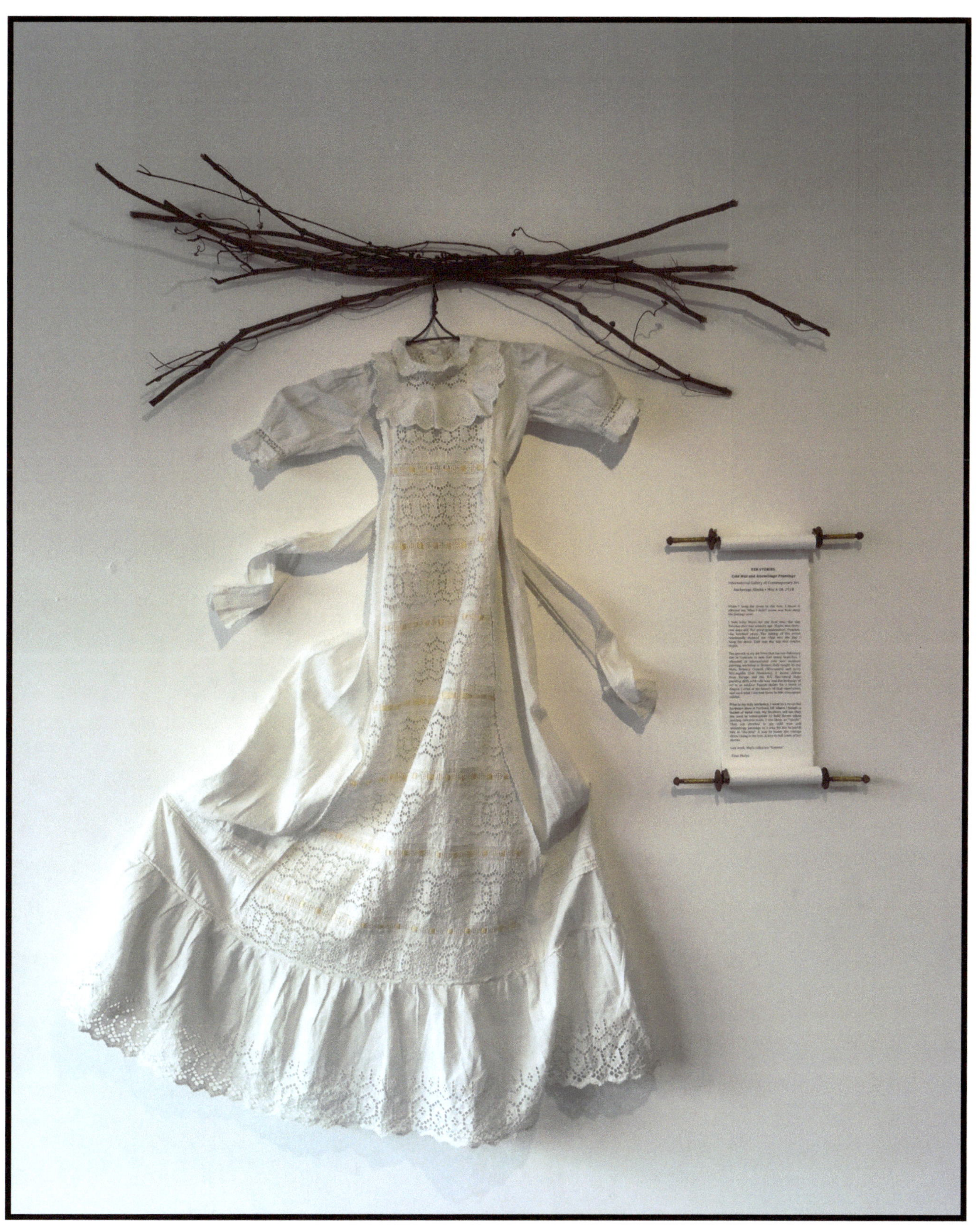

WELCOME TO THE EXHIBIT

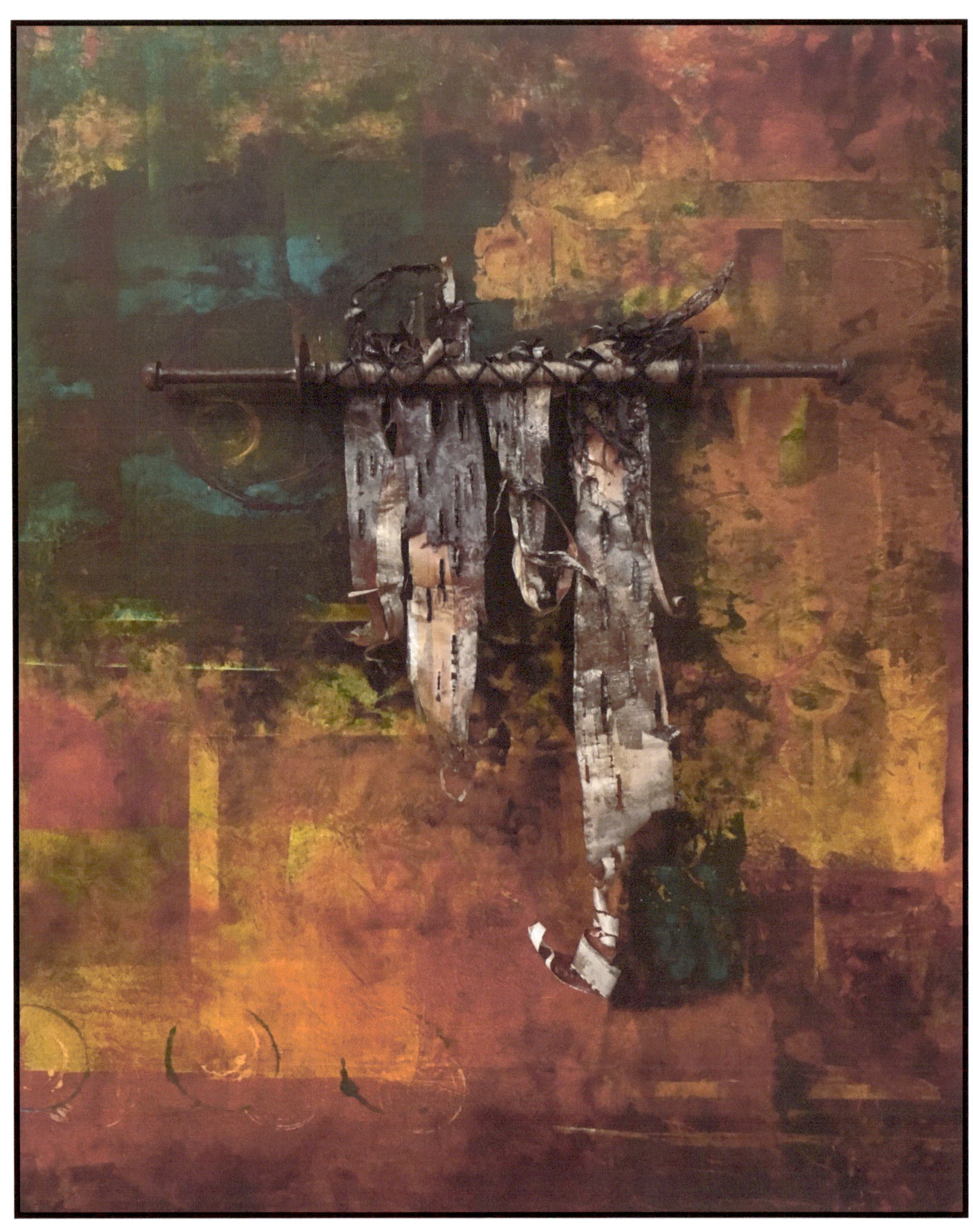

UNDER HER SKIN

UNDER HER SKIN

"Like water off a duck's back," she said.
Our school counselor was amazing—for children and teachers. She shared her advice
with me early in my teaching career after a difficult meeting with a parent. I thought
about her words over the years as I became a more experienced teacher. I became more
confident. Developed a thicker teaching skin.

Now, as a full-time artist, it can be difficult to put my work out there. I feel vulnerable.
Exposed. My art is part of me. At first, I hoped everyone would like my art, was
crushed when they didn't. As though I had done something wrong. Now I have a
thicker art skin. My confidence as an artist develops in layers like the skin of the birch
bark attached in this painting.

My back still gets wet a little, sometimes, but I'm getting there.

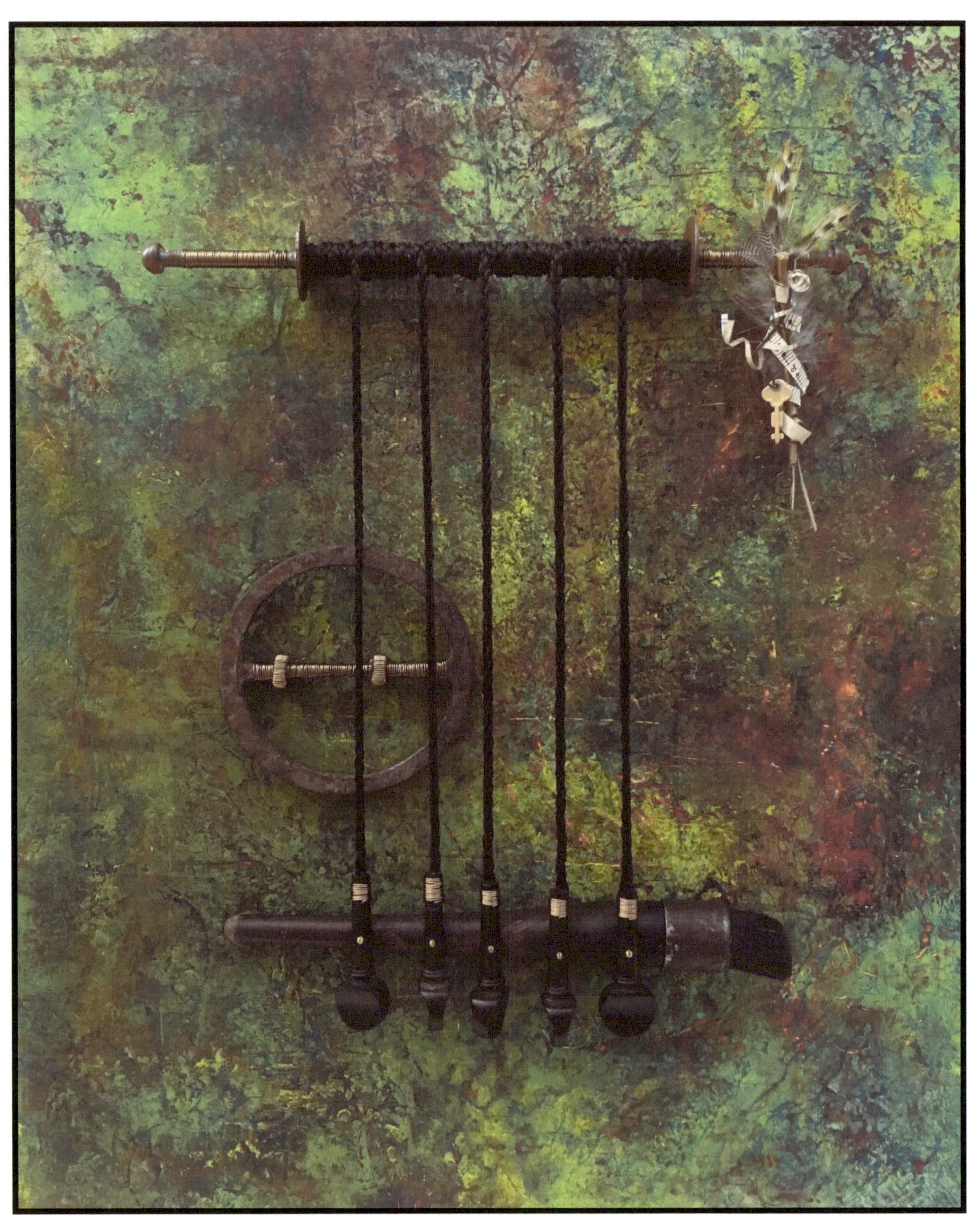

HER MUSES

HER MUSES

Included in this work are:

—Some of my hair
—Vintage paint brush
—Tuning pegs
—Vintage metal
—Key
—Wire
—Feather
—Bits of sheet music
—Memories

In school, each of us kids played an instrument, encouraged by my dad. Sue and John played sax, Jay trumpet, Jim percussion, and flute for me. Now I am an artist, like my mother with her creative eye for making things of beauty with so little. These memories are now my muses.

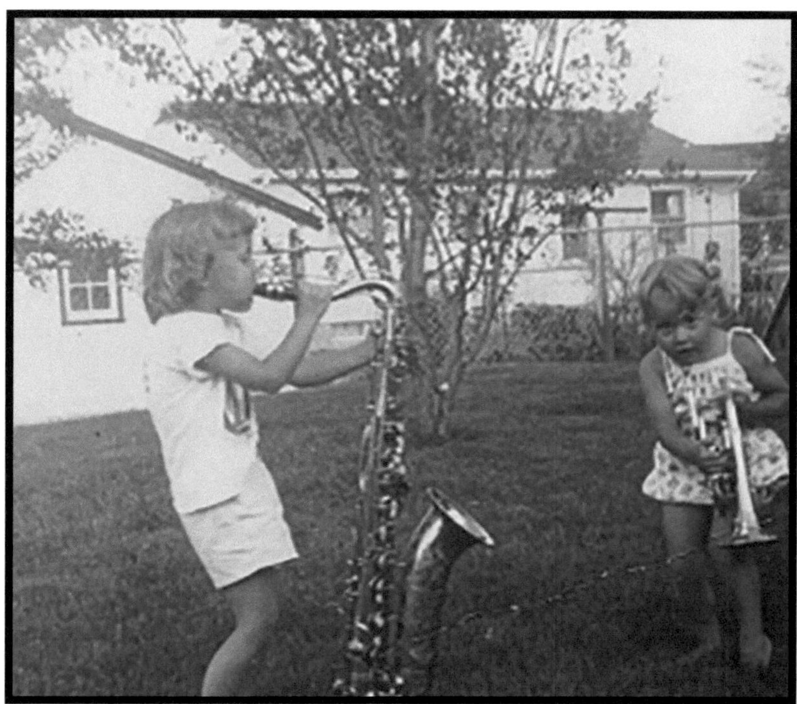

Big sister, Sue, and me, playing instruments

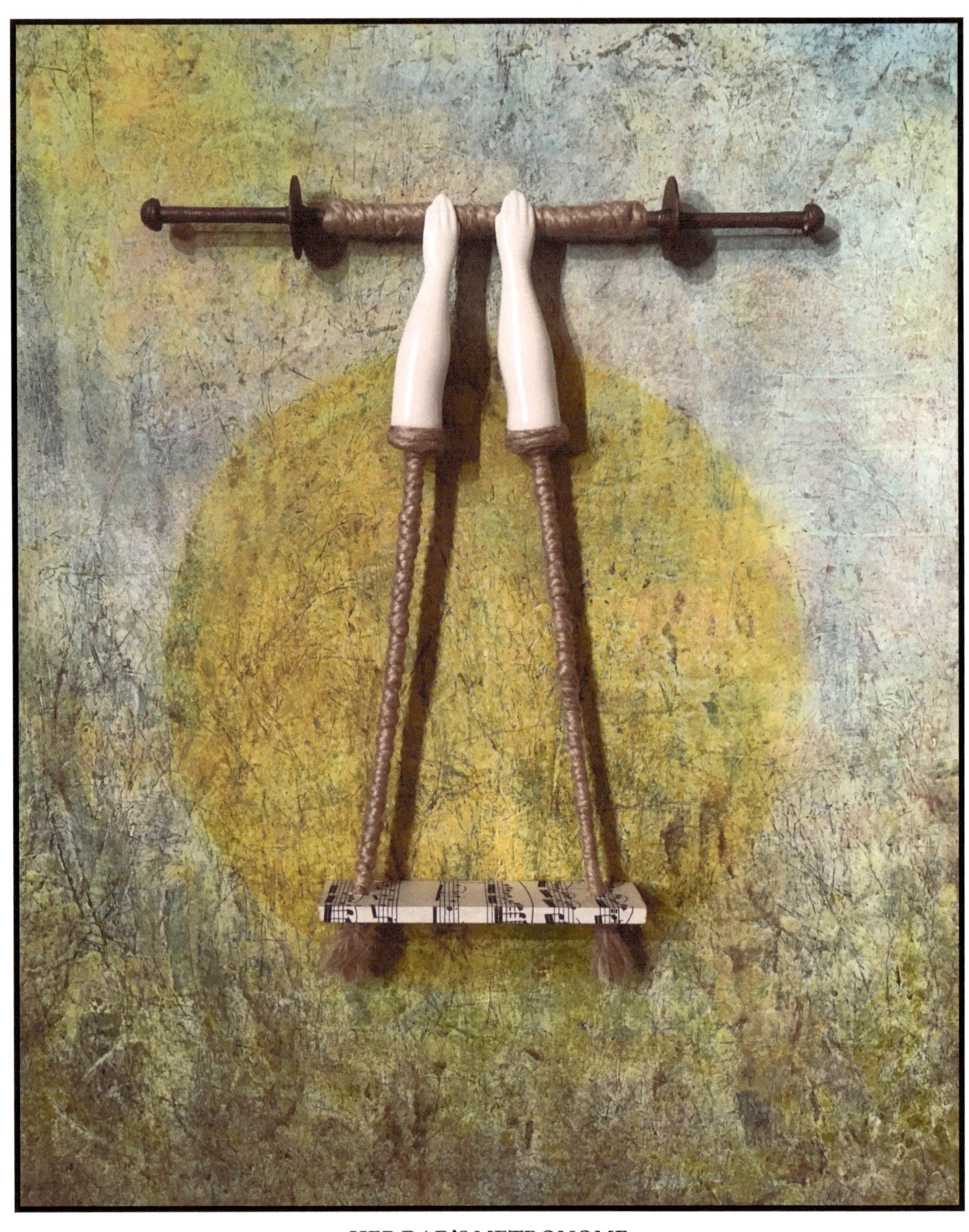

HER DAD'S METRONOME

HER DAD'S METRONOME

When I was six, I was going to join the circus and be a "type-rope" walker, thanks to my musician dad, Sid Phelps. He made rope swings for us five kids in every backyard we had growing up, from Nebraska to Colorado to Alaska. One swing was inside our house. I became very good at tricks on the ropes. Once, after a huge night windstorm in Sidney, Nebraska, I woke up to the delight of our sunny backyard filled with tumbleweeds. A beautiful sight to behold. I made my way to the rope, held it tightly, climbed up the fence to the narrow top ledge. I used this fence ledge as my runway before I swung bravely out and around the *sea of danger*. Toes pointed. After my swoop above the tumbleweeds, I delicately landed, running expertly along the two-by-four fence ledge to continue my daring *circle of death performance*, over and over and over. Each time I imagined how my sparkly fringed costume (with fishnet stockings) looked to the crowd. I could hear the roaring applause. I thought about what my stage name would be.

I can't help but think of the satisfaction and joy my dad must have had watching each of us kids, and sometimes mom, as we rhythmically swung like a metronome on the rope swings he made for us.

Through this painting, "Her Dad's Metronome," I hang onto, and share, the warm memories of sunny skies, family, and joys of long ago.

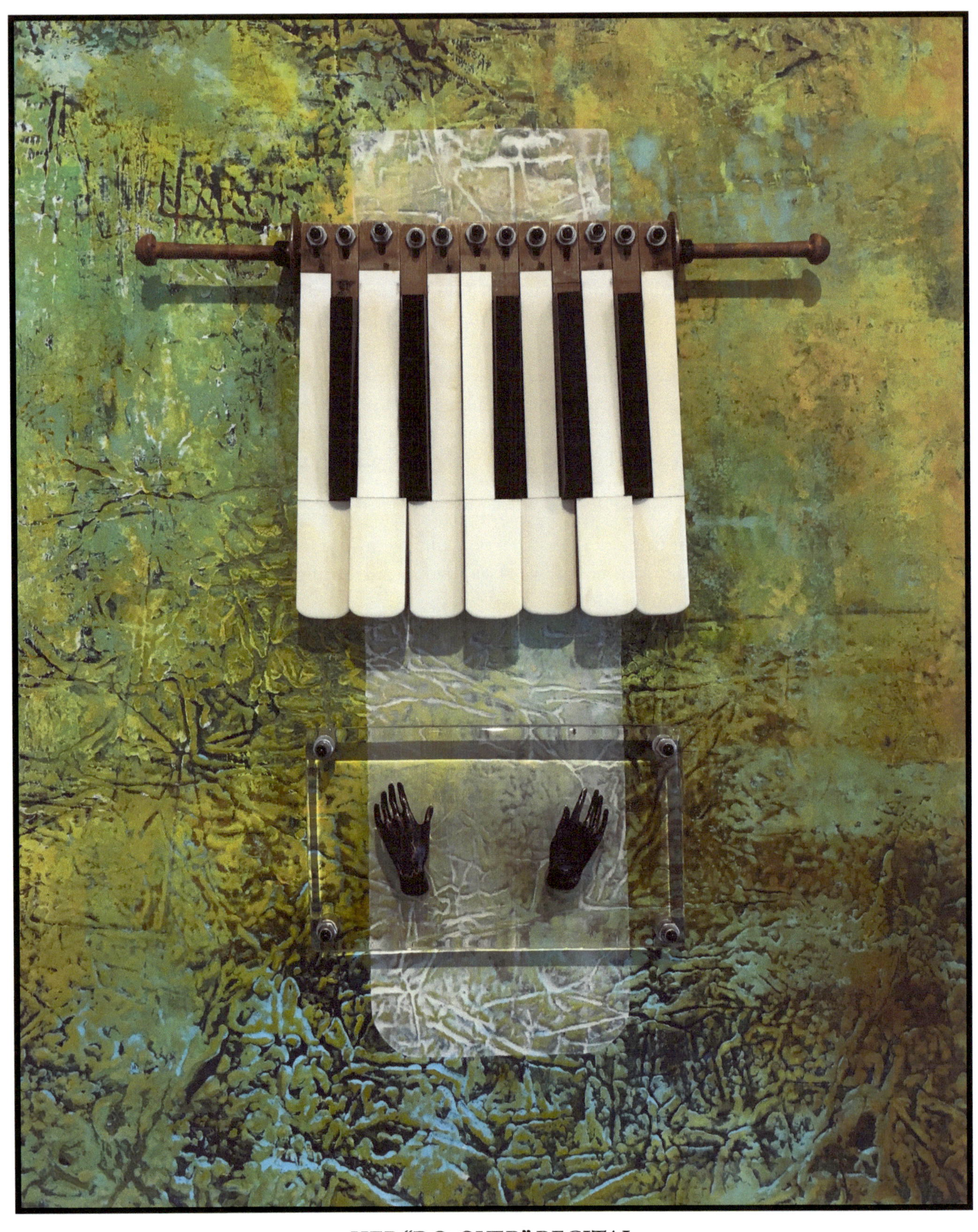

HER "DO-OVER" RECITAL

HER "DO-OVER" RECITAL

Dad had a music store in Greeley, Colorado, next door to Maudie's head shop. My sister was 14 and I was 12. We lived to be groovy. It was 1969. Our visits to "see dad" at his store were really opportunities to swoon over the older teenage guitar players and drummers who would jam there on occasion. Sometimes dad let us choose guitar picks for our growing collection before we'd go next door to wonder at the strange wares at Maudie's.

I decided one day I wanted to take piano lessons. At dad's music store. Perfect. We had a player piano at home. The kind where you put a music roll in, pump the pedals, and voila! Piano music. That was pretty much my idea of practicing on the piano.

For my first piano recital, I wanted to play "Yesterday," "Leaving on a Jet Plane," or "Angel of the Morning." My piano teacher, Mary, had other plans: "Rocking Horse Swing." I can still hear that piece in my head. Don't like it any more now than I did then. Not what I'd call groovy, hence it did not make it to the top of my practice list.

The big recital day arrived at dad's music store. I didn't know how to play "Rocking Horse Swing." I wanted the floor to open and swallow me. Excruciating embarrassment in front of everyone, especially my dad. I do have to say I learned a lot taking piano lessons, and even learned a little bit about how to play the piano.

By making this piece of art, "Her 'Do-Over' Recital," I made peace with my 12 year old self. And hopefully my dad.

Feelin' groovy.

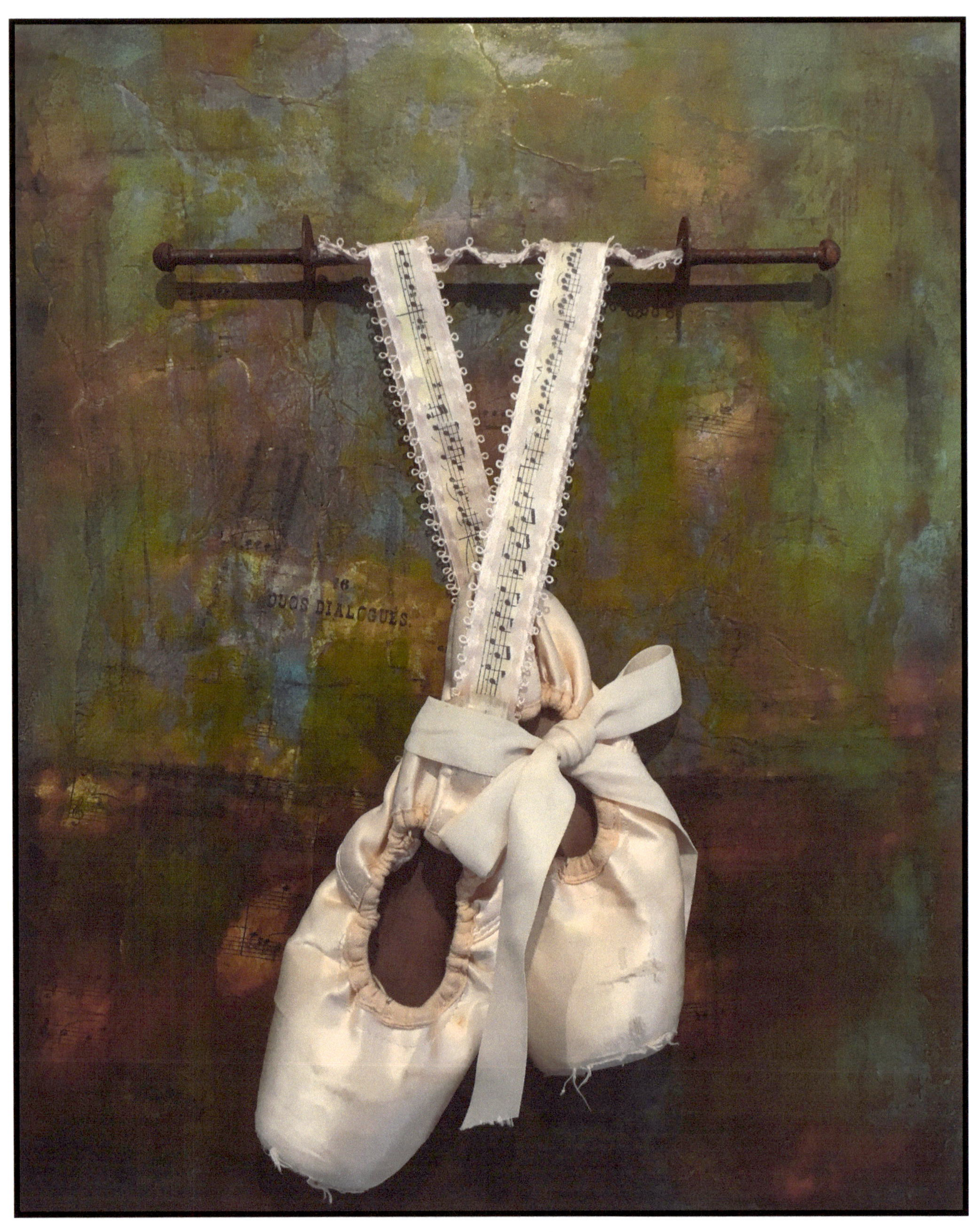

MUSCLE MEMORY

MUSCLE MEMORY

PROPERTY OF ROMIG JR. HIGH, ANCHORAGE was stamped on the copy of the sheet music I found in a folder of my treasures that were at least 50 years old. I figured because it was a copy and not an original, it was OK to use it in my artwork. So far, I have not been arrested.

16 – "Duos Dialogues" is the name of the music piece placed safely under the pigment, wax, and pointe shoes in my *Muscle Memory* painting. This piano piece is much like the treasured thoughts of my forever friend, Jakki. She and I were a strong flute duo through Junior and Senior high school, with Jakki sitting first chair and me second. Her position was indisputable. She went on to play with the symphony, and she, too, is now an artist.

If I were to mention "Mary Funk's School of Dance" to my big sister, Sue, she would break into a tap dance of "shuffle-ball-change, shuffle-ball-change, shuffle, shuffle, shuffle-ball-change." Thanks to our mom, Ardis Phelps, who signed us up for dance lessons, my sister and I became a loving duo long, long ago. We still do that tap dance together. We talk on the phone almost every day.

I used to dance on my toe knuckles in preparation to become a ballerina. That changed over the years, and I became a gymnast instead. My circus dreams as a performer had run off, but I remained a duo with my mind and body.

I still play the flute. I've been known to dance. And flexibility is still my friend. Jakki will always be my forever friend. Sue is the best sister anyone could ever imagine. Safely placed under the layers of my life are treasured muscle memories from long ago.

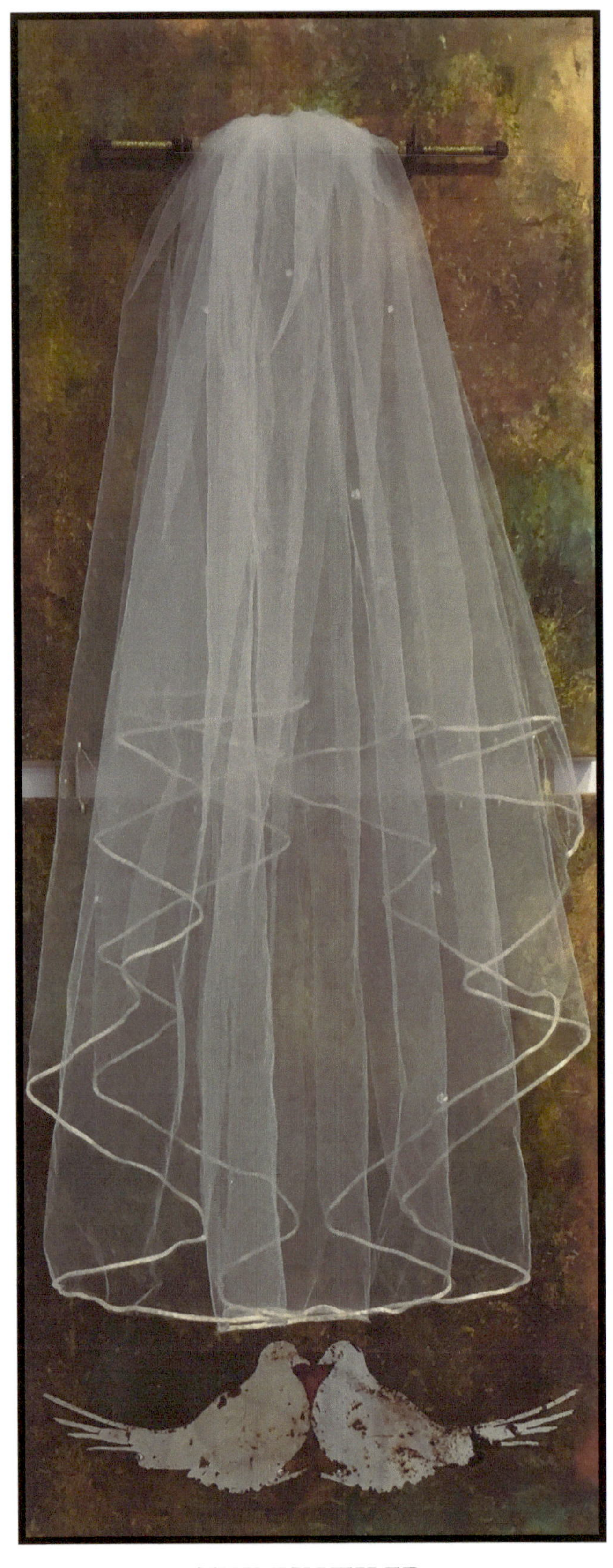

THINLY VEILED

THINLY VEILED

A girl's wedding. She looks lovely, radiant. They face each other and the unknown. If you looked behind the veil on this diptych painting, you would see gold thread trying to hold the two pieces together long ago. Love stories can become thinly veiled episodes of unspoken truths, some sweet, some bitter, as their lives unfold.

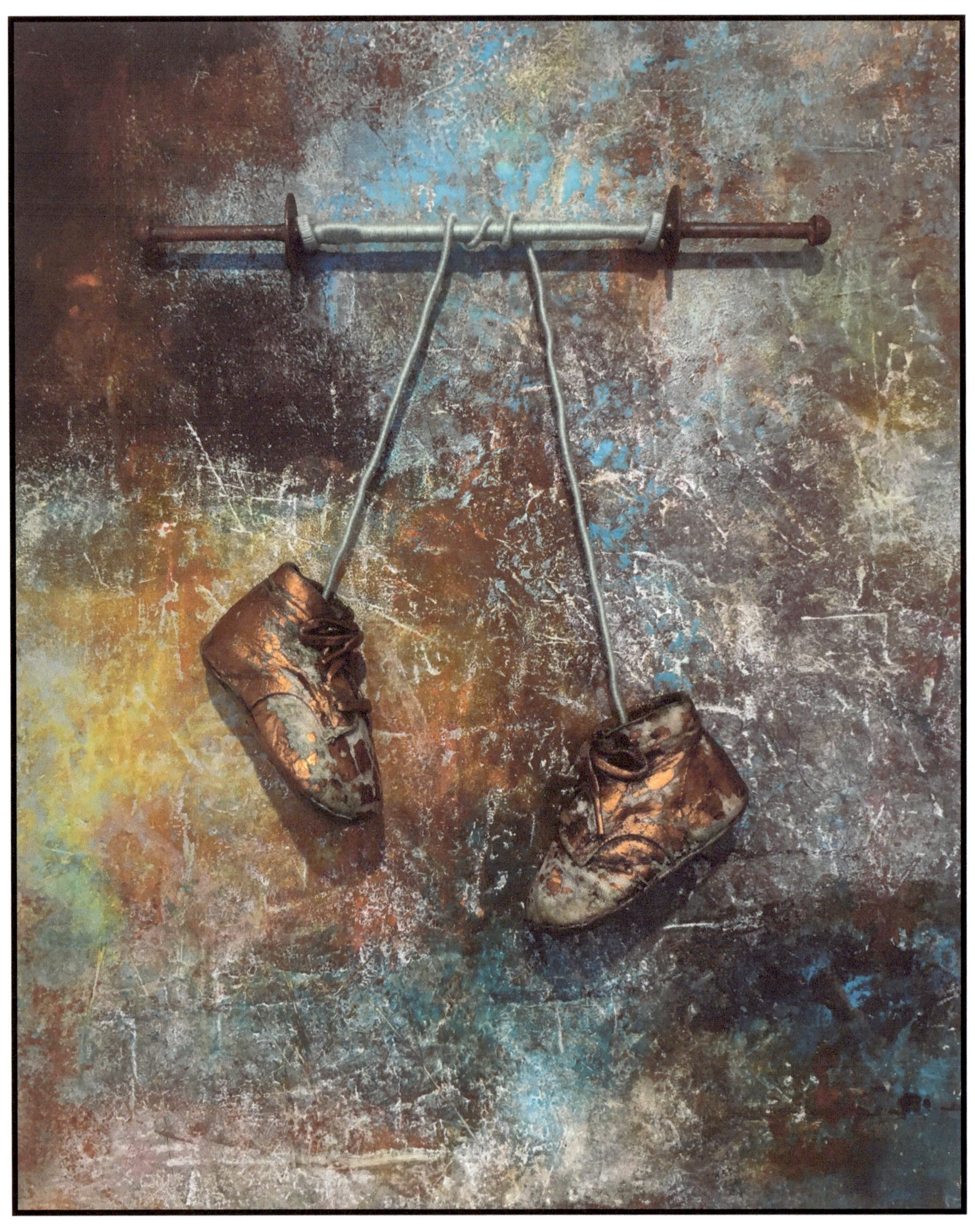

COULDA BEEN A CONTENDER

COULDA BEEN A CONTENDER

 As I gathered my art for this book, I was reminded of the sadness I sometimes experience as a woman who has not had children. I haven't really set out to make art specifically about this feeling, but it seems to have organically evolved that way in parts of my last four collections. I am just going with it. And I might not be done. Not having children was not by choice. It just didn't happen. And that's okay. I woke up recently with my Medicare card, a wonderful husband, no children, and a creative passion that defines me, makes me happy, gives me tremendous joy. The iconic girly/feminine symbols I use in some of my artwork seem to be my current way of expressing this journey, in part, as a cathartic experience, but also with a focus on female beauty and an opportunity to offer respect for human beings without judgment or knowledge of their past. It feels like a possibility for shared growth when I communicate this awareness through art. "Coulda Been A Contender" makes me think of a boxer who has hung up the gloves. I accept and share this facet of the surprise journey called life and move forward.

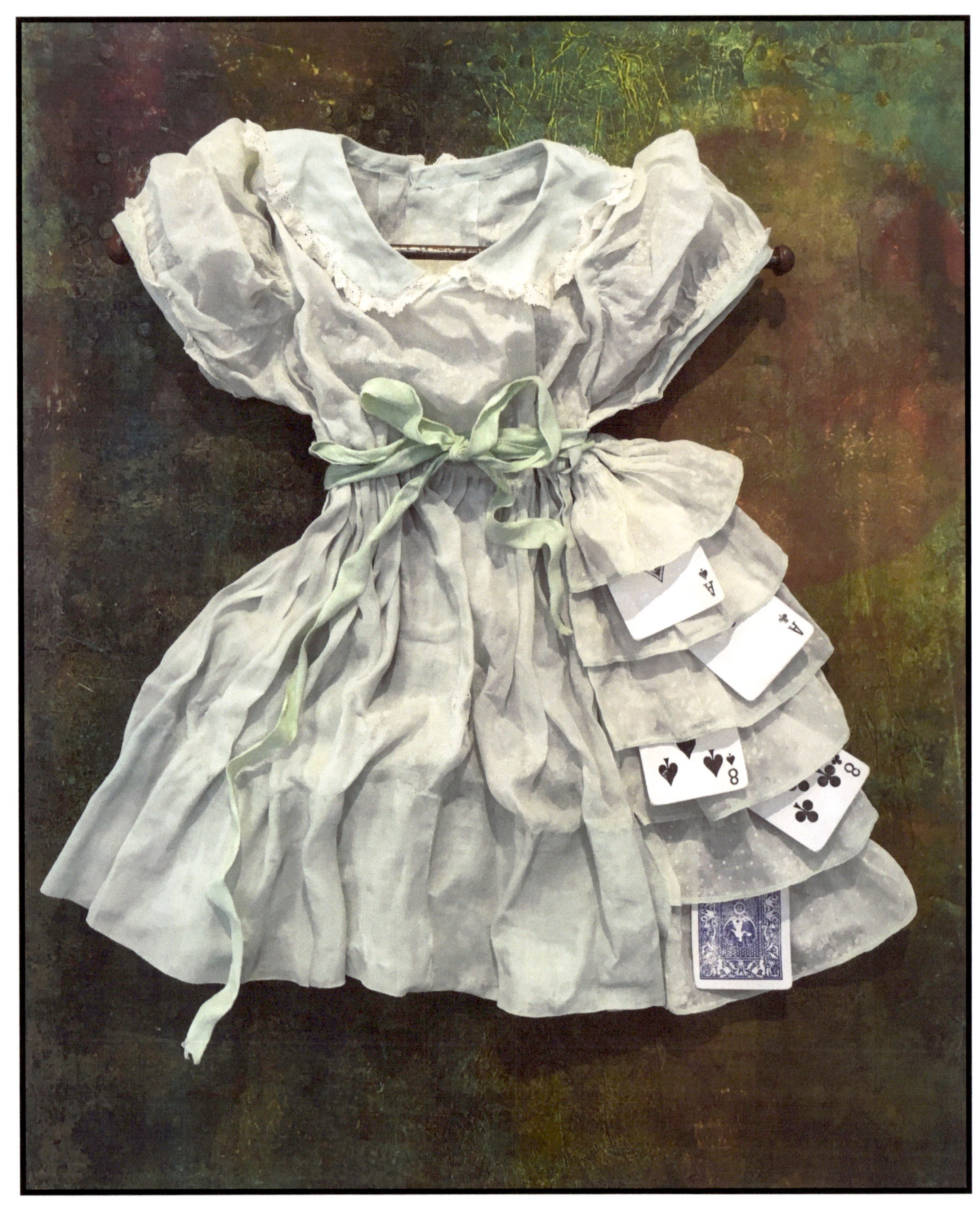

QUEEN OF HEARTS

QUEEN OF HEARTS

I really like the person in this piece of art. I'd like to be more like her. Feisty. Don't mess with her. She holds, hidden in ruffles, the key to her life, and mine: the Queen of Hearts. Love.

Wild Bill Hickok wrote of love in the unsent letter to his wife the day before he held his final poker hand at Saloon No. 10 in Deadwood, South Dakota: "Aces and Eights"—forever now known as "The dead man's hand."

My family has been known to lift a glass in the Number 10 Saloon in the Black Hills of South Dakota.

Here's to the Queen of Hearts.

(The unseen card in this painting is the Queen of Hearts. There is disagreement about the fifth hole card Wild Bill held.)

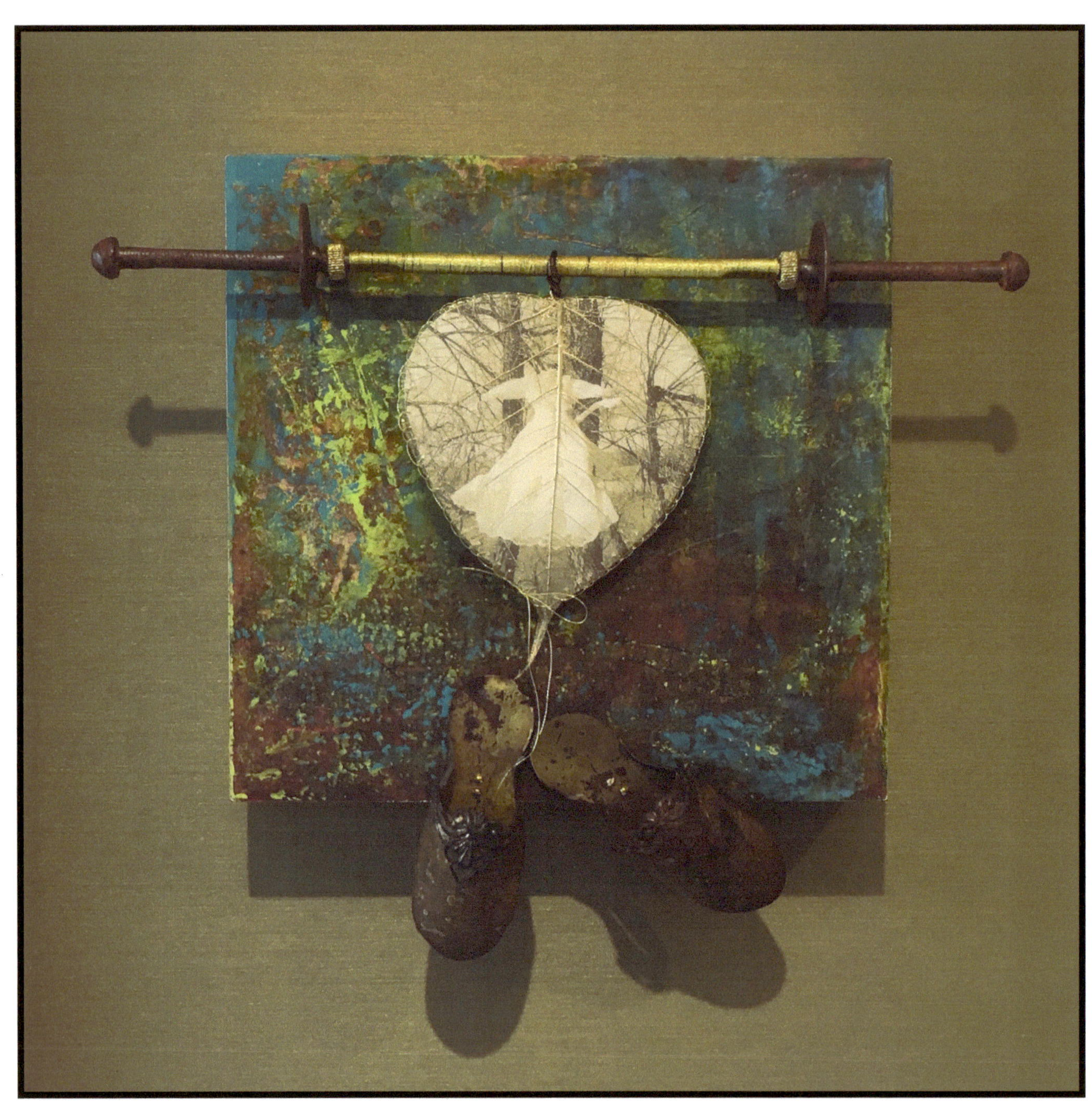

HER FINAL WALTZ

HER FINAL WALTZ

Kerry's mother, Peaches, loved to dance. Especially a waltz, or a two-step. She could even "Charleston." She did a boy's work on her father's homestead in eastern Montana in the 1920s and 30s before completing a two-year teacher's degree, teaching in a one-room rural school in Montana, then her B. Ed., and M. Ed. Her professional name was Kathyrn Marie (Hauk) Feldman.

Her parents, Mike and Kate, met at a dance in Perham, Minnesota. Mike was 19, and Kate was 16. They danced all night; he took her home in a horse-drawn buggy. A year later, he took her as his wife on a train to Montana (a poem about that train ride occurs earlier in this book: "Riding A Train West"). When they were invited to appear on Valentine's Day on the "Good Morning America" show to be interviewed by David Hartman, Peaches flew with her parents to the Big Apple. It was their 75th wedding year. David Hartman asked the secret of living happily for 75 years in marriage. Gram Kate told him, "We met at a dance, we dance every Saturday night, and never go to bed angry." They had eight children. Peaches was their second child.

I think Peaches would smile to know this is how I remember, honor, and miss her, as I hear her whisper again, "I like you." Her first words to me after we met.

III

GROWING PANES:
REFLECTIONS ON AN AMARYLLIS

Photographs by Richard J. Murphy
Art and Introduction by Tami Phelps
Text by Kerry Dean Feldman

Introduction

When Richard Murphy finished photographing the amaryllis one Alaska winter, he said the work felt "undone." When he offered his photos to me for consideration, to use as I wished for my art, I was amazed and honored. I knew then we had the framework for a mixed media art story. The collaboration seed was planted.

Without any planning or discussion ahead of time, we created a collection of six pieces of art using photography and mixed media, each of us telling a similar story. A story of love and loss. Of beloved women in our respective lives, told through the metaphor of an amaryllis.

Each individual piece in this section of our book tells a story. Collectively they are a life-cycle story of "woman." Richard eloquently explains his story about our collaboration and some of his photographic techniques in his artist statement at the end of our book. I made the art piece, "Remembering," specifically in memory of my mother, Ardis Phelps, who suffered and died from early onset Alzheimer's at age 63.

Cold wax medium, oils, acrylics, watercolors, cloth, resin, dried flowers, my favorite hand-colored photograph of my sister, Sue, and me, and a variety of found objects are some of the materials used in my artwork. Plexiglass "panes" that I found earlier were used to present Richard's photographs, which explains the title, "Growing Panes: Reflections on an Amaryllis."

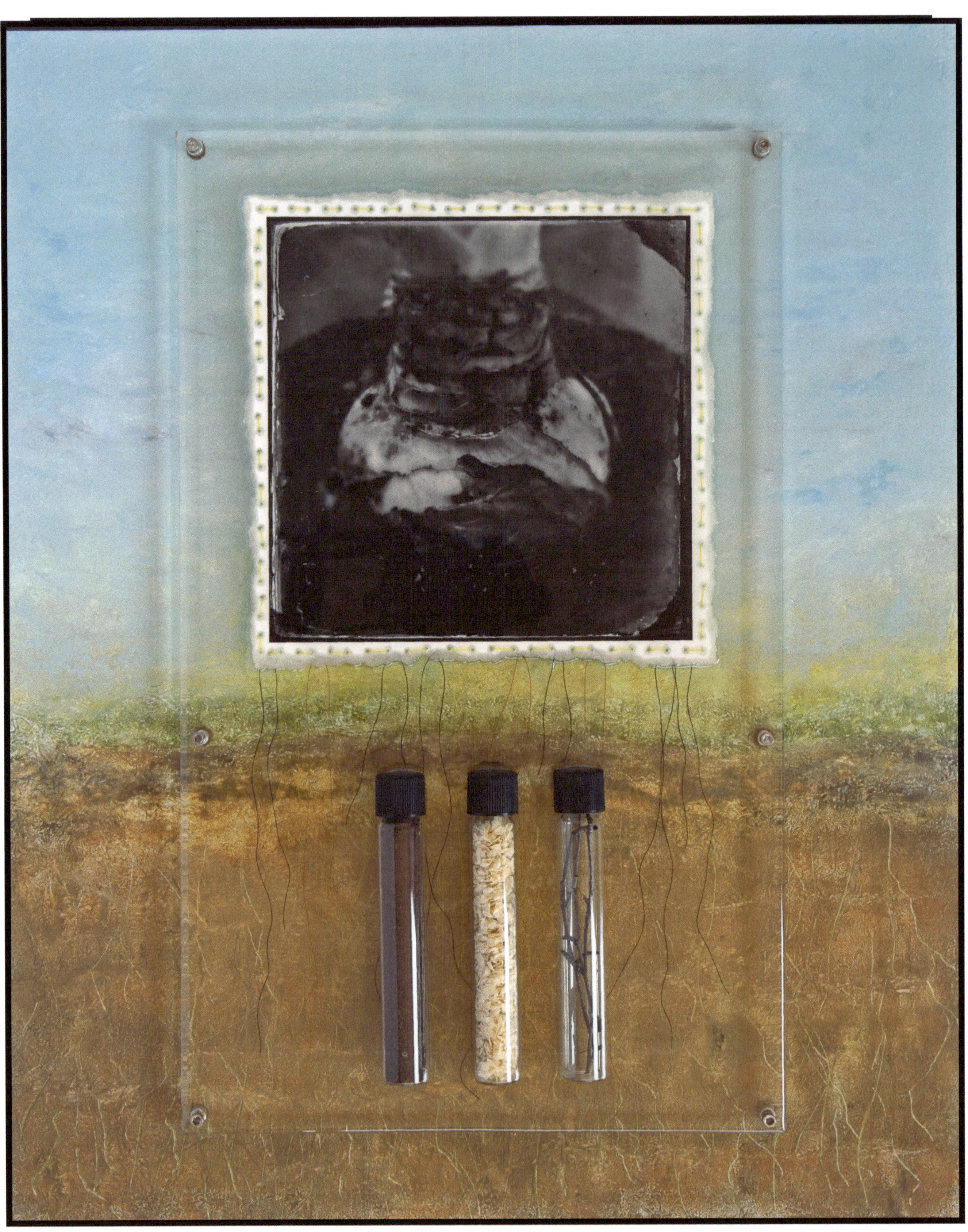

SOWING
a flower,
like a child,
has roots

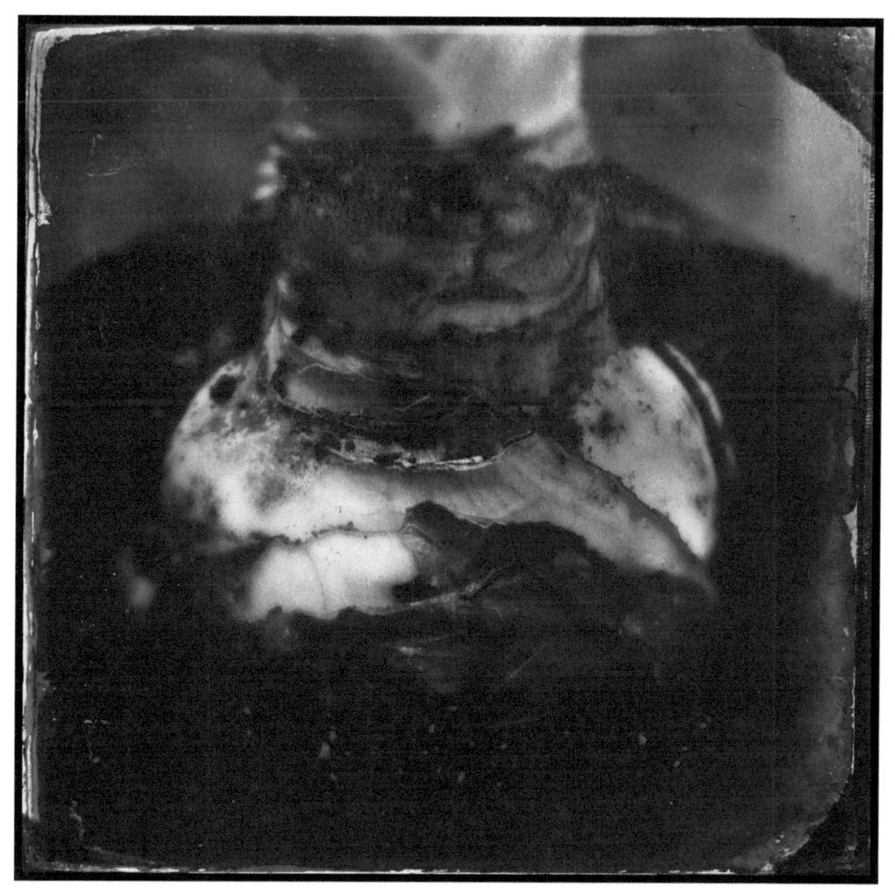

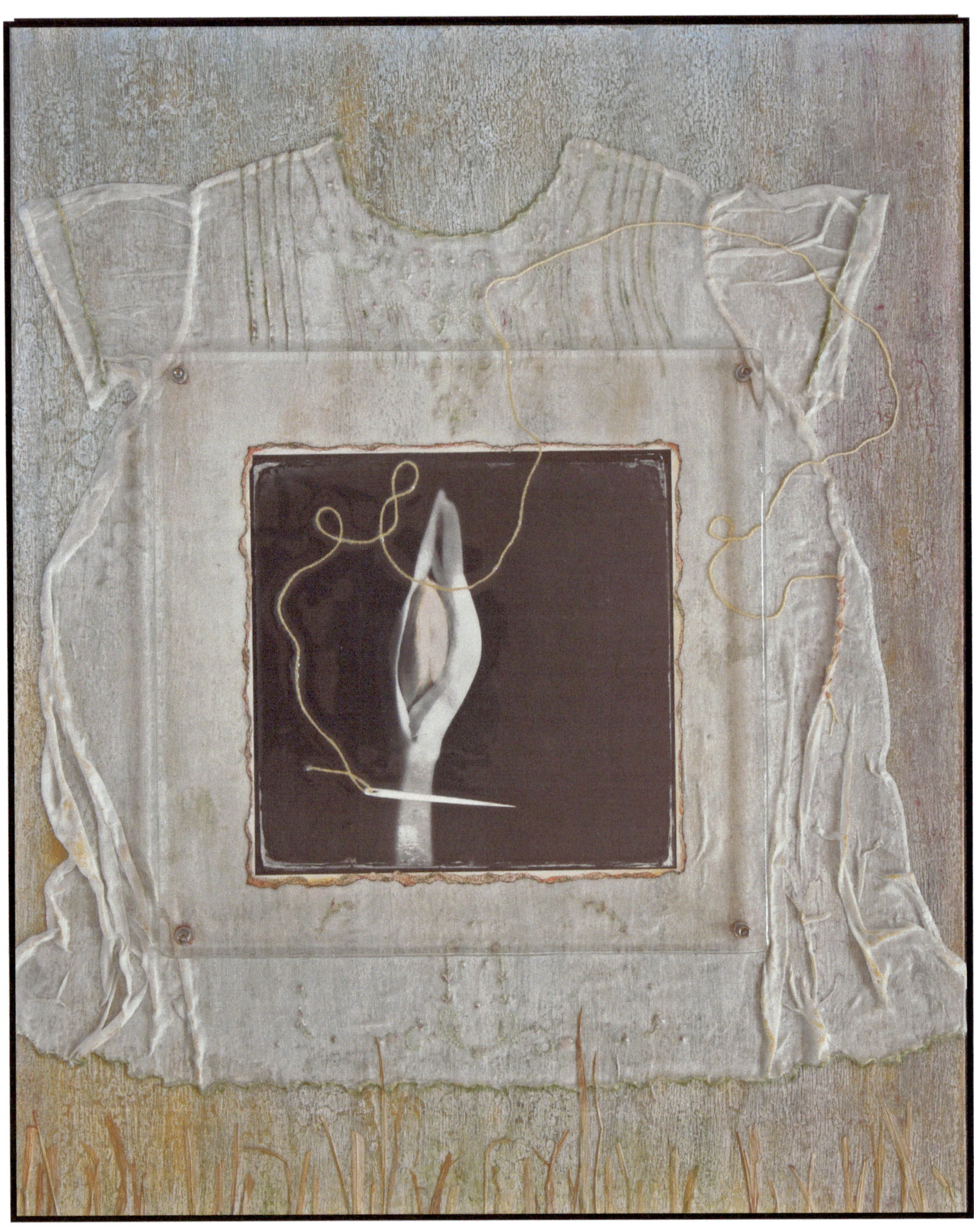

BEGINNING
a girl's beginning,
womanhood awaits

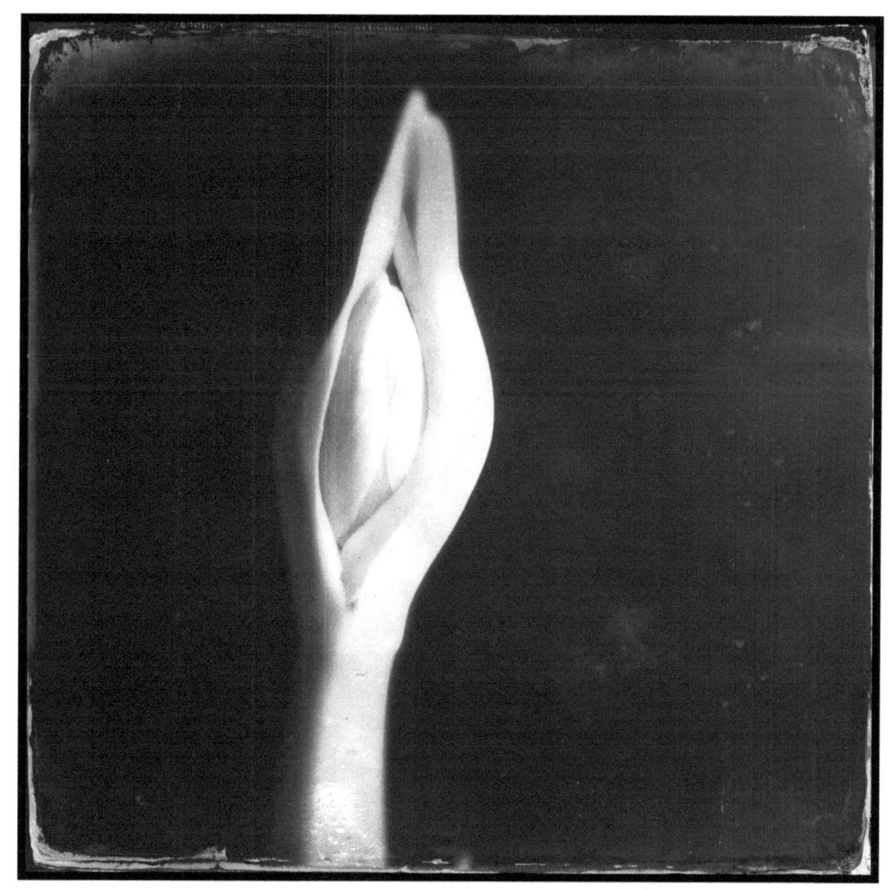

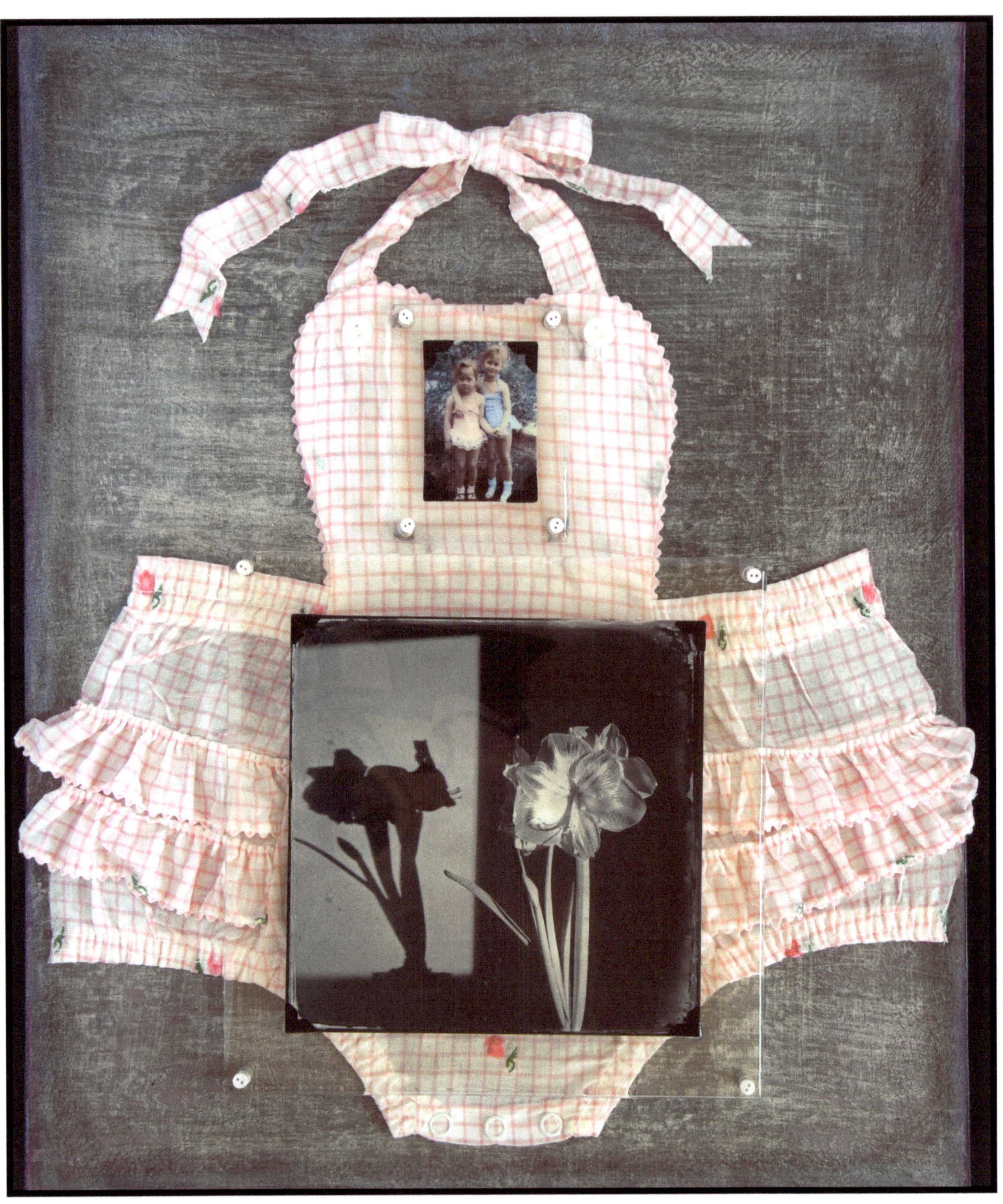

SHADOWING
a big sister can guide
a girl
in becoming a woman

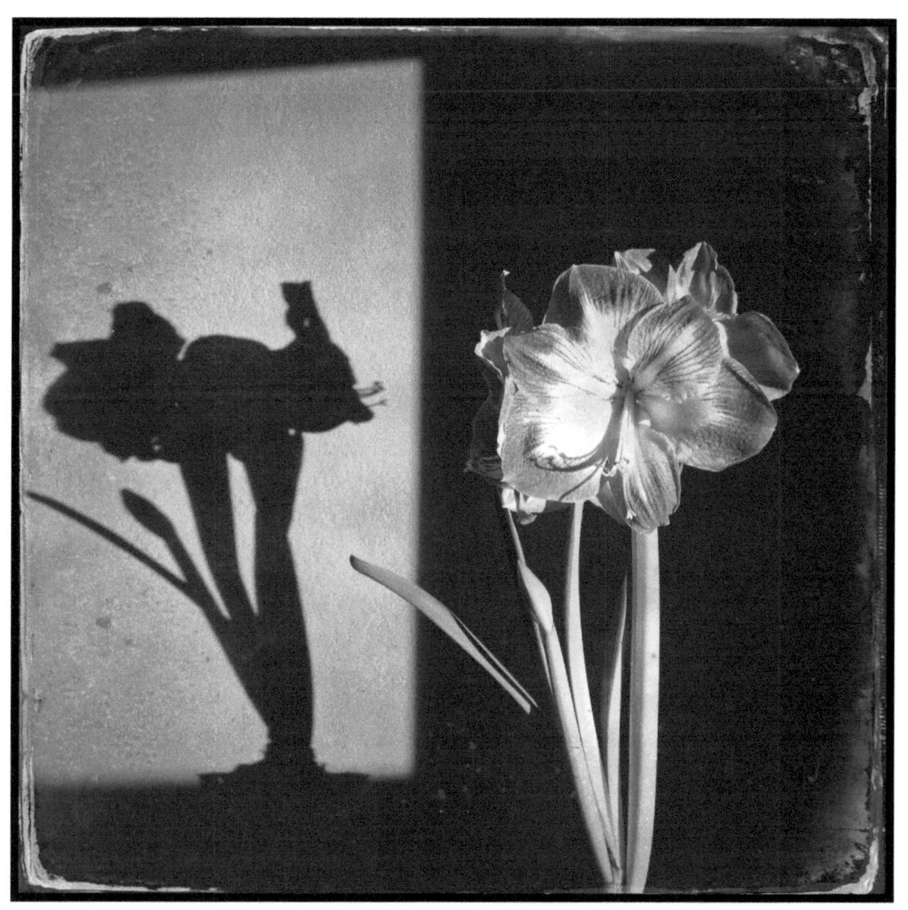

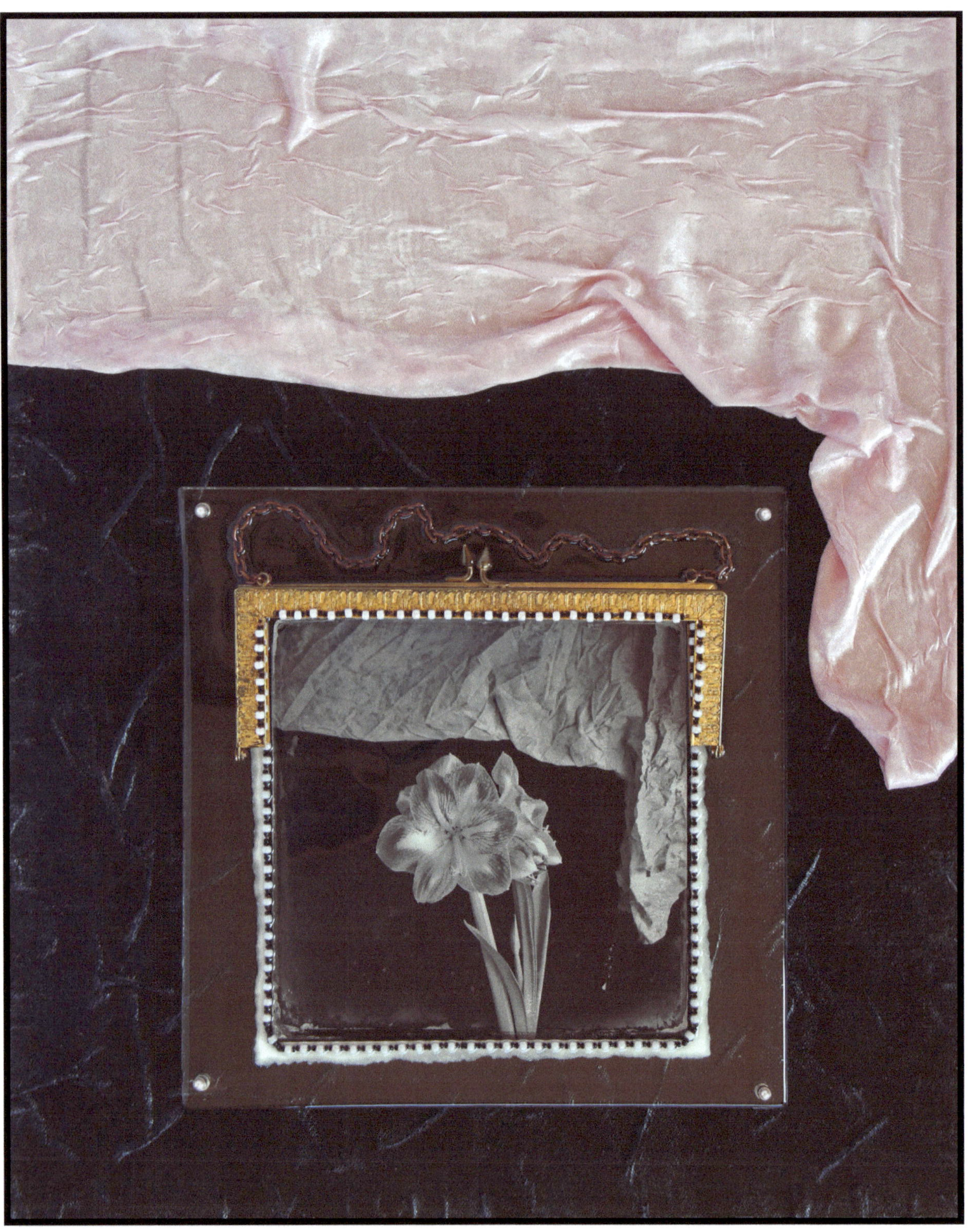

BECOMING
*a girl's first date
blossoming,
becoming*

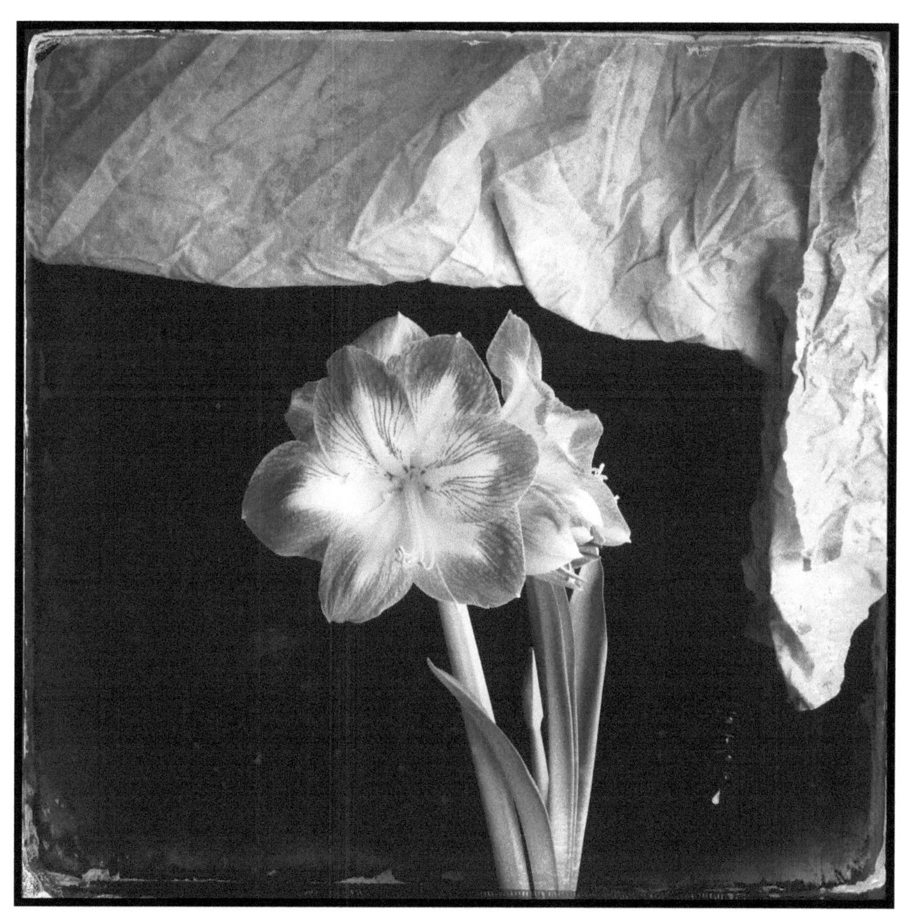

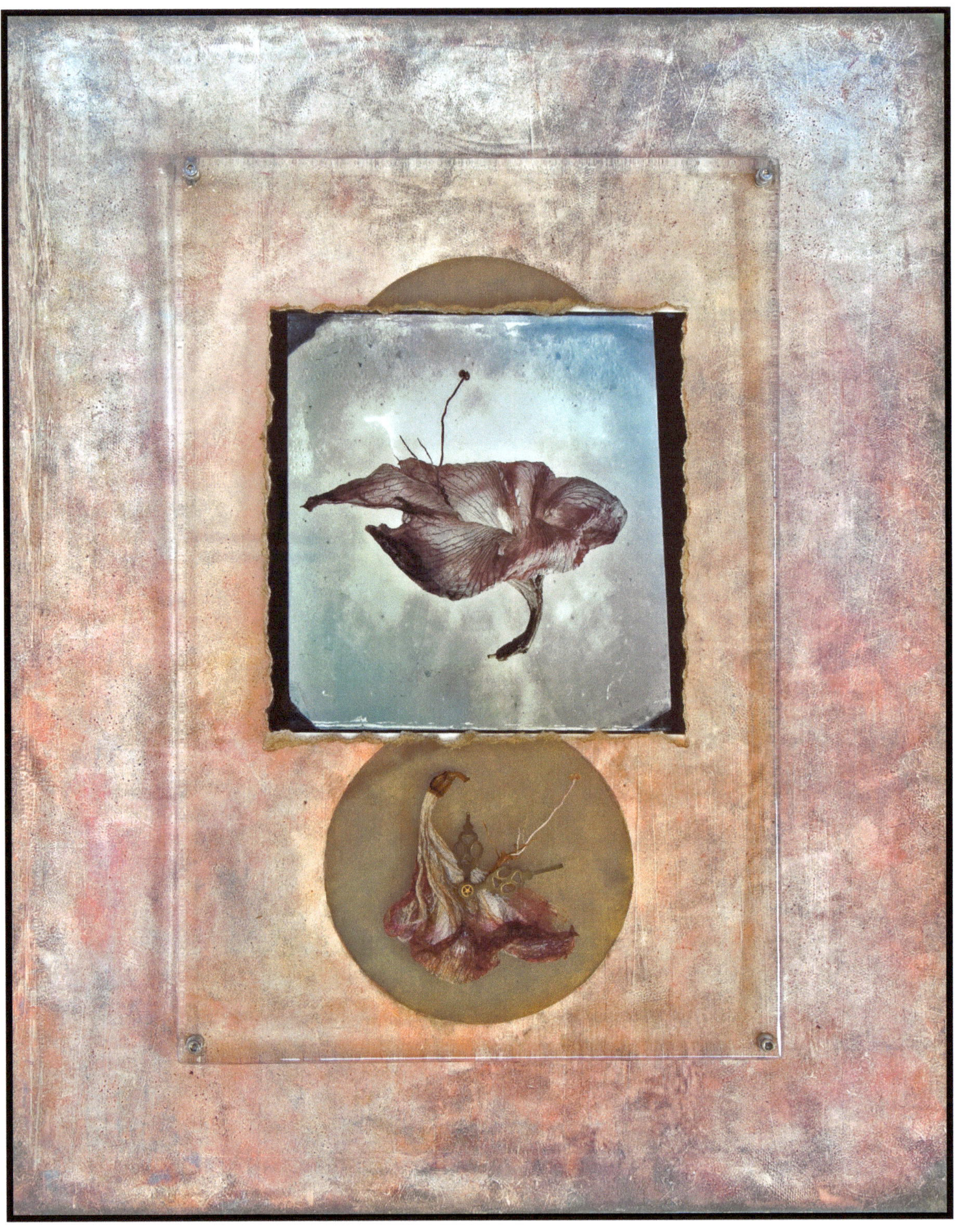

84

REMEMBERING
a woman in transition,
time bound,
her clock life ticks,
beauty, mystery

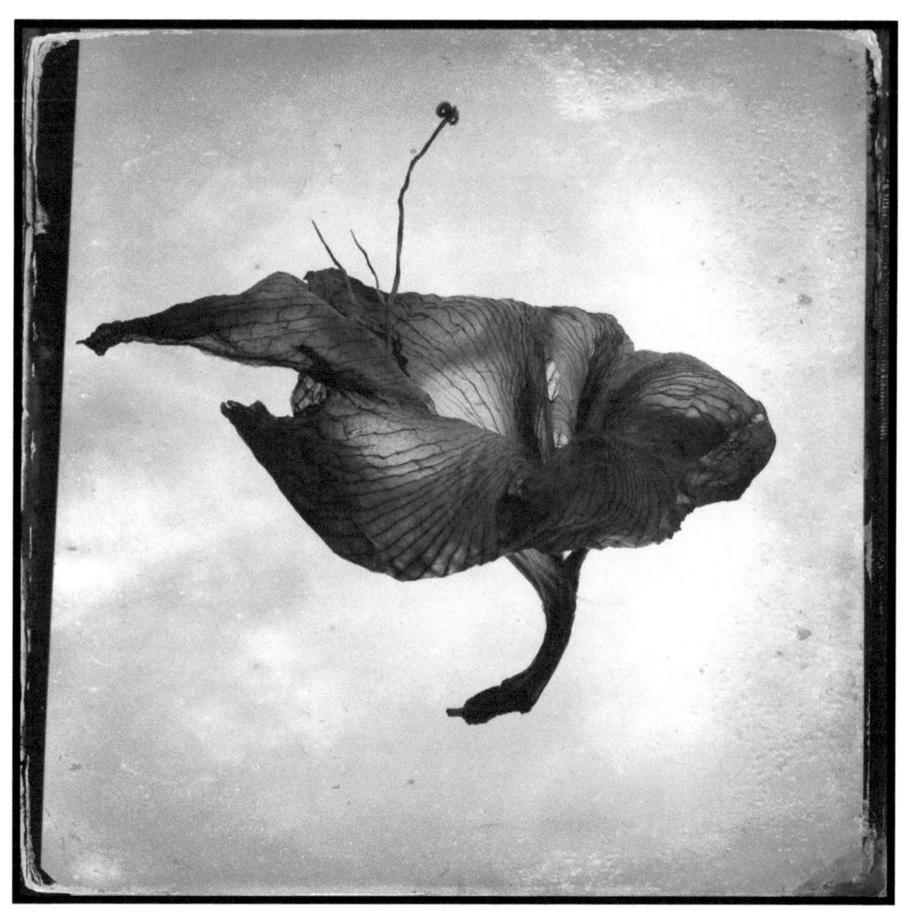

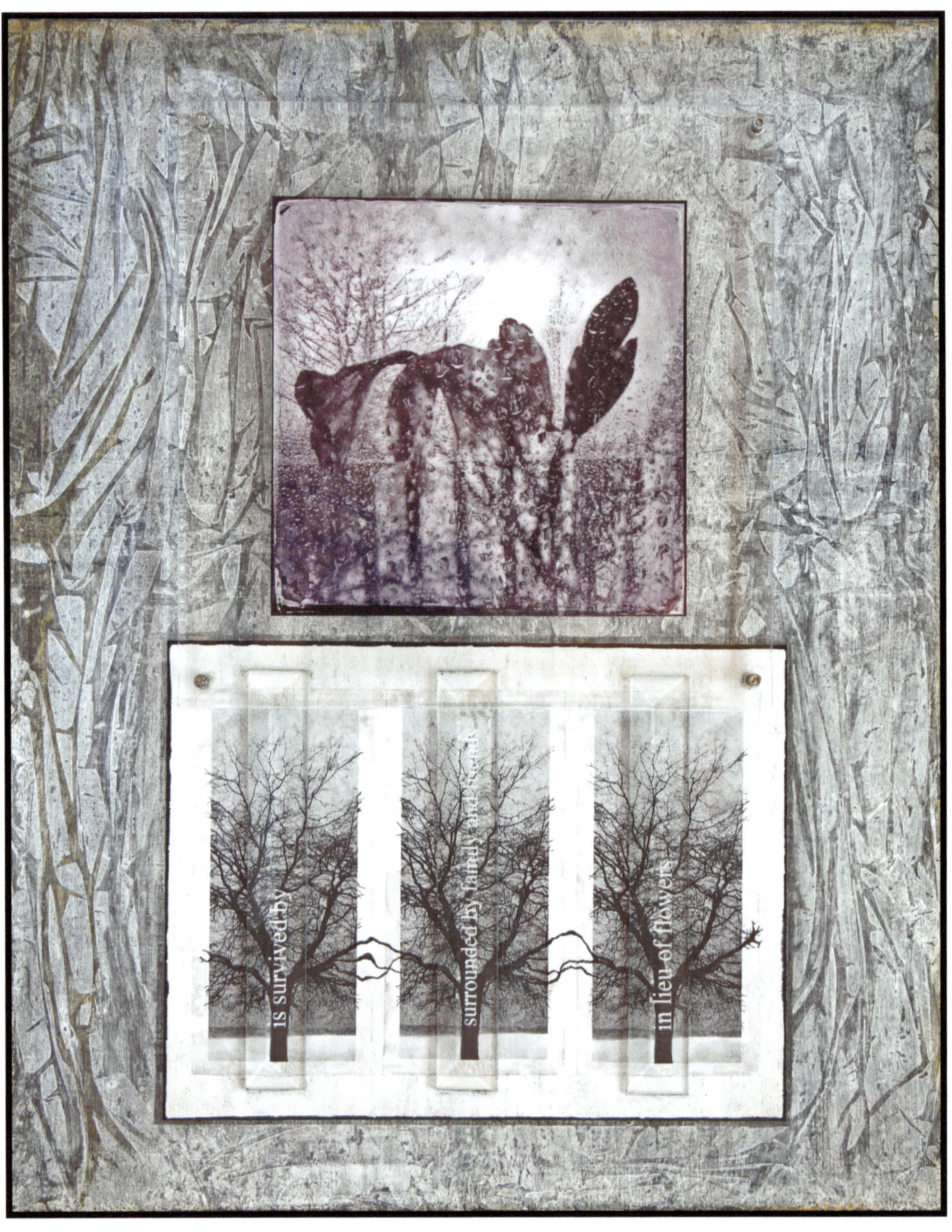

is survived by
surrounded by family and friends
in lieu of flowers

ENDING
when she's gone,
always remembering,
aching,
only silence

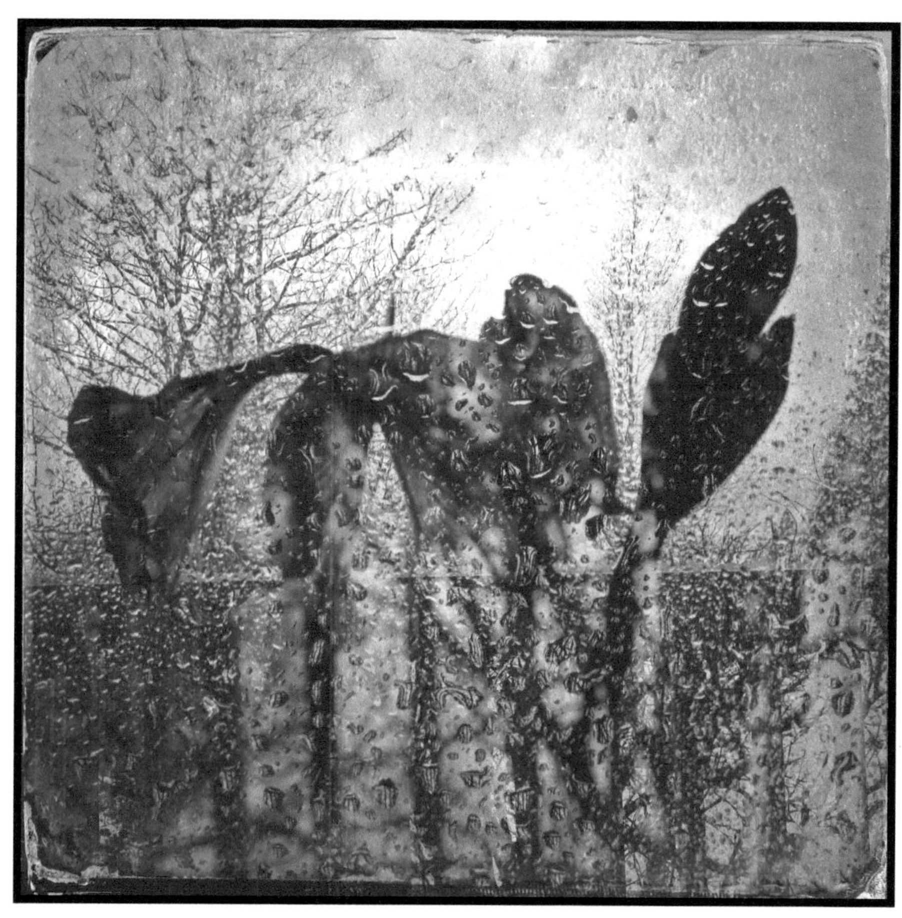

IV

PLEASED TO MEET YOU

Self -Portrait Sculpture and Text by Tami Phelps

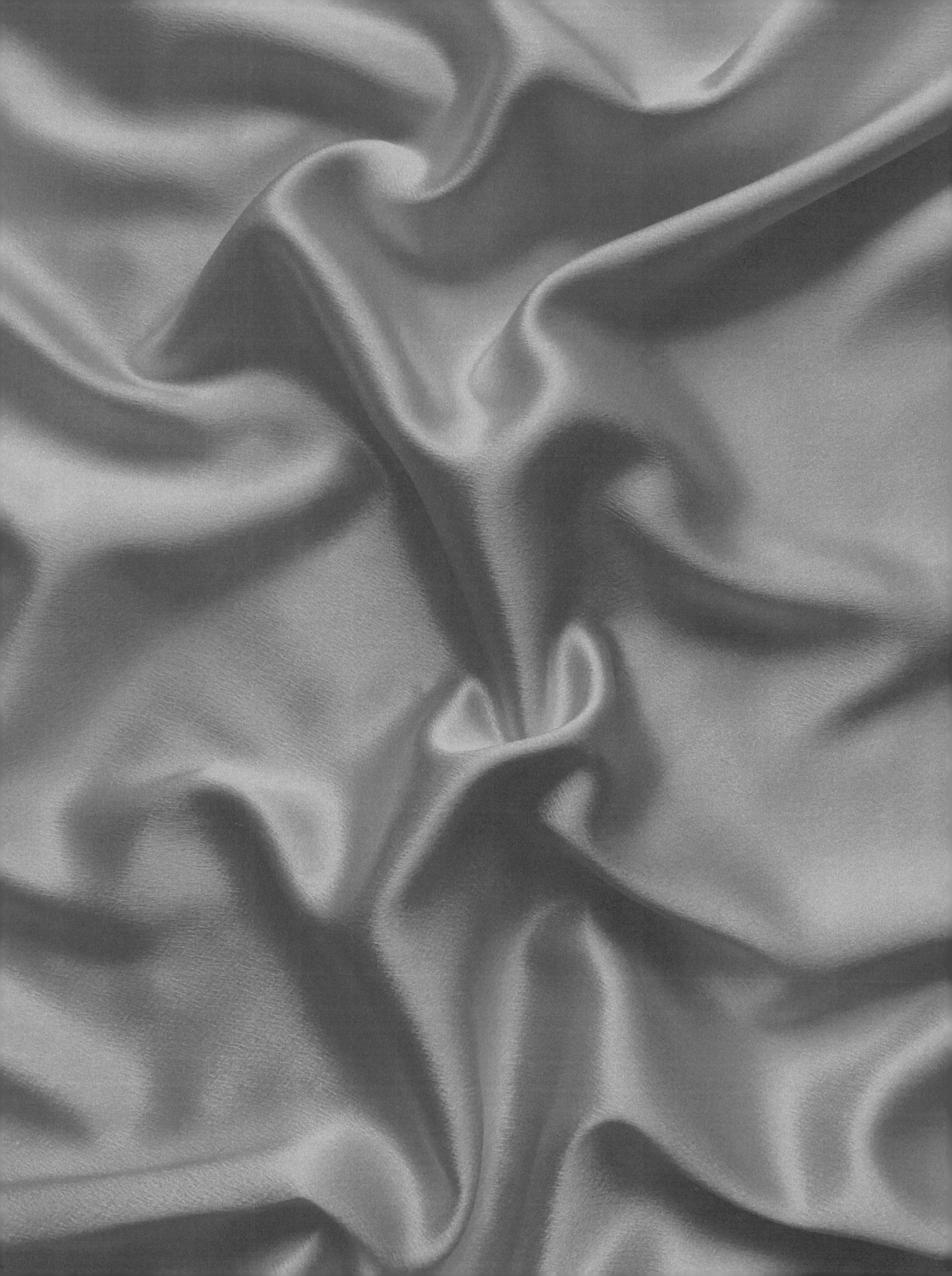

PLEASED TO MEET YOU

A friend of mine gave me the beautiful christening dress she wore as a baby. She knows I make artwork with baby dresses and said she wanted me to have it to use as I wished in my art.

Years later, with gratitude, that tiny dress was part of a sculpture on exhibit in the Hugh McPeck Gallery, 2022, at the University of Alaska Anchorage.

My sculpture, "Pleased to Meet You," was juried into the exhibit by international artist, Indra Arriaga Delgado, in the 37th Annual Self-Portrait National Competition of Limited Size. Each piece of art in the show could not exceed 12 inches in any direction.

I tailored the baby dress to fit the armature of a lampshade that was the perfect size. Plaster painted molds of my hands gently cupping a hollow egg on a nest of my hair are visible inside the "womb" of the dress, which represents my mother. A view from the top of the sculpture further portrays the lifecycle of "female" through the hand-sewn fabric I fashioned as the portal to fertility and birth.

I know my friend did not imagine this for the future of her christening dress, nor did I. It is my hope that she is as pleased to meet it as I am to have made it.

It seemed fitting to end our book with art about a woman within a woman.

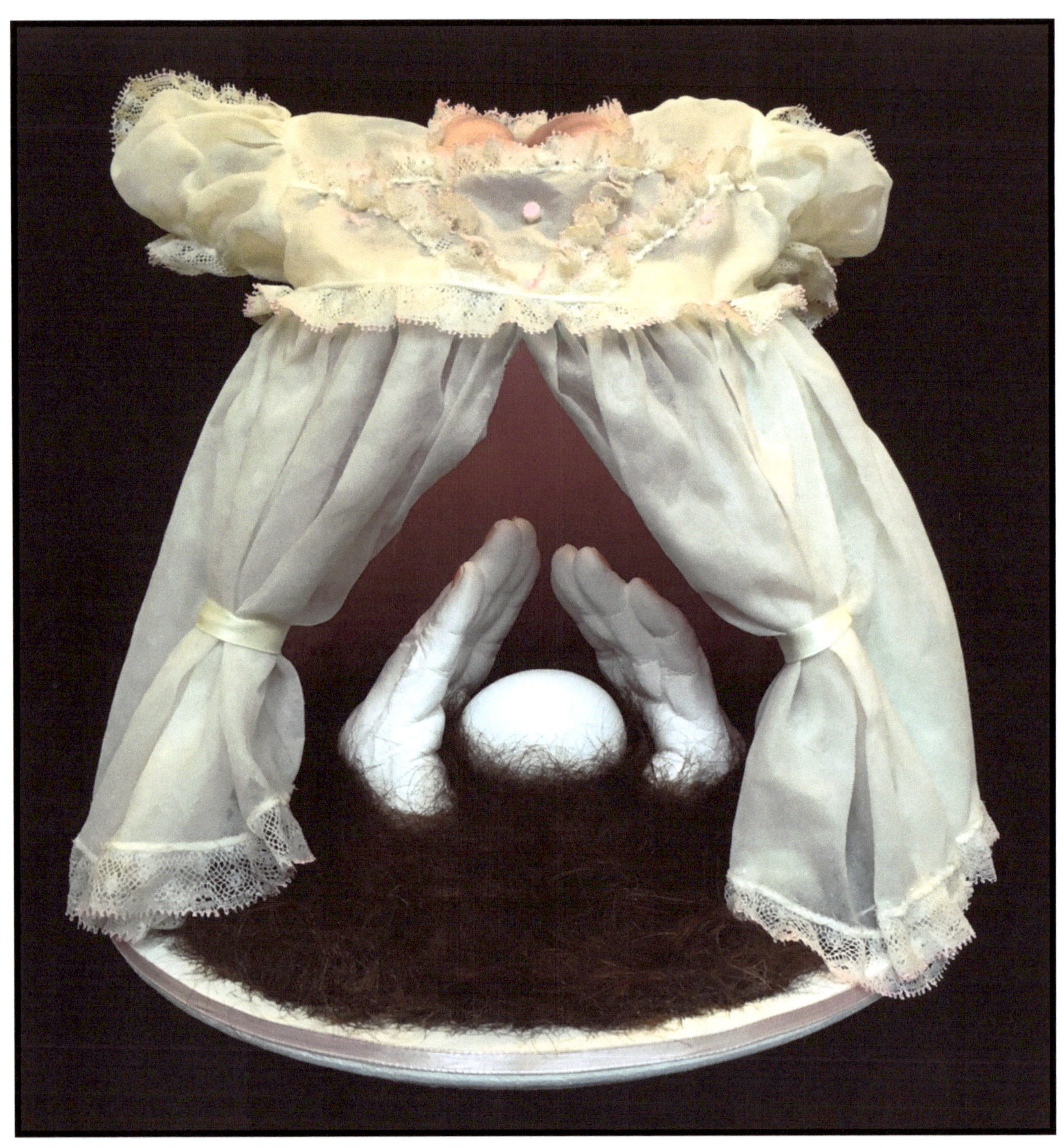

PLEASED TO MEET YOU

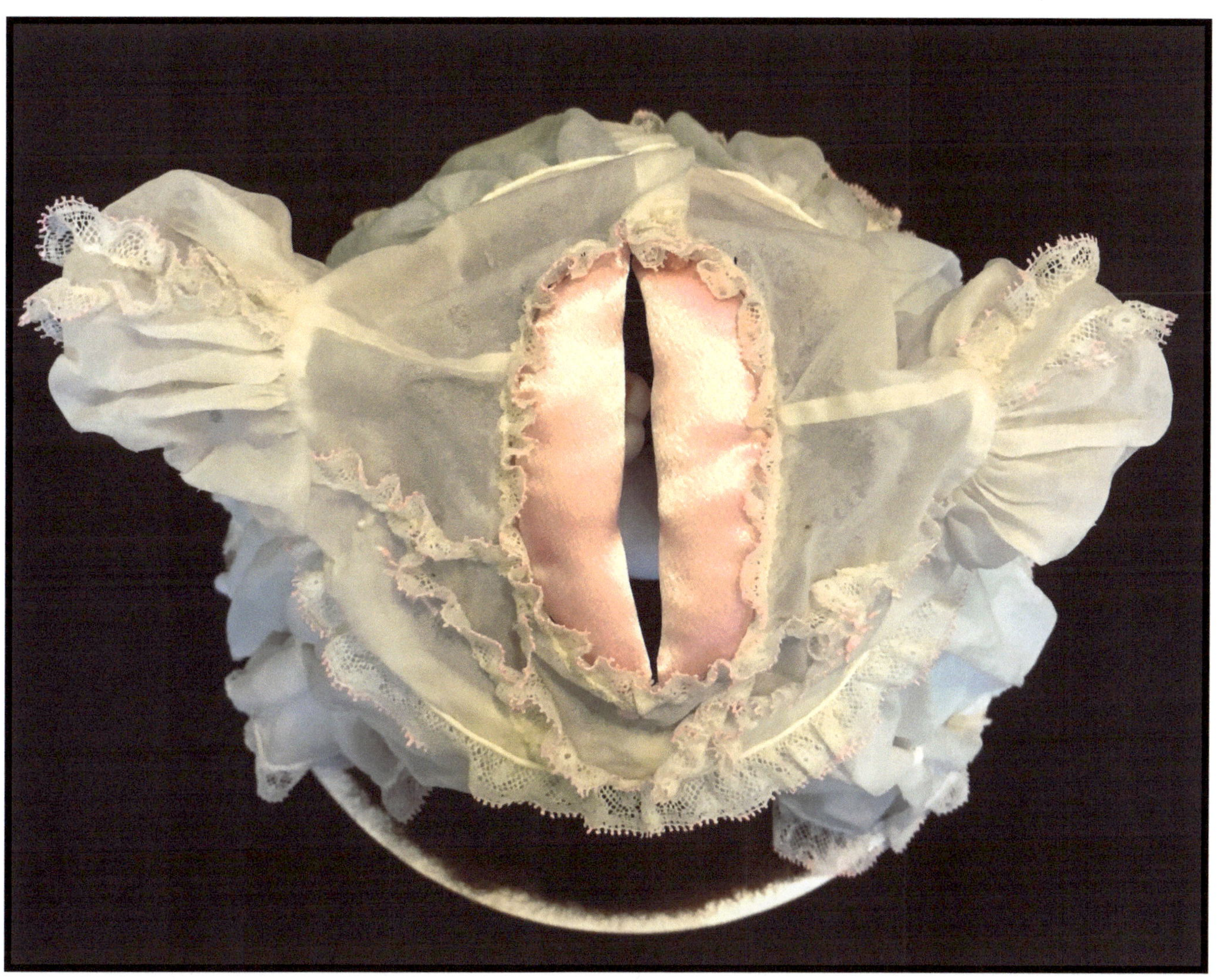

(Top View)

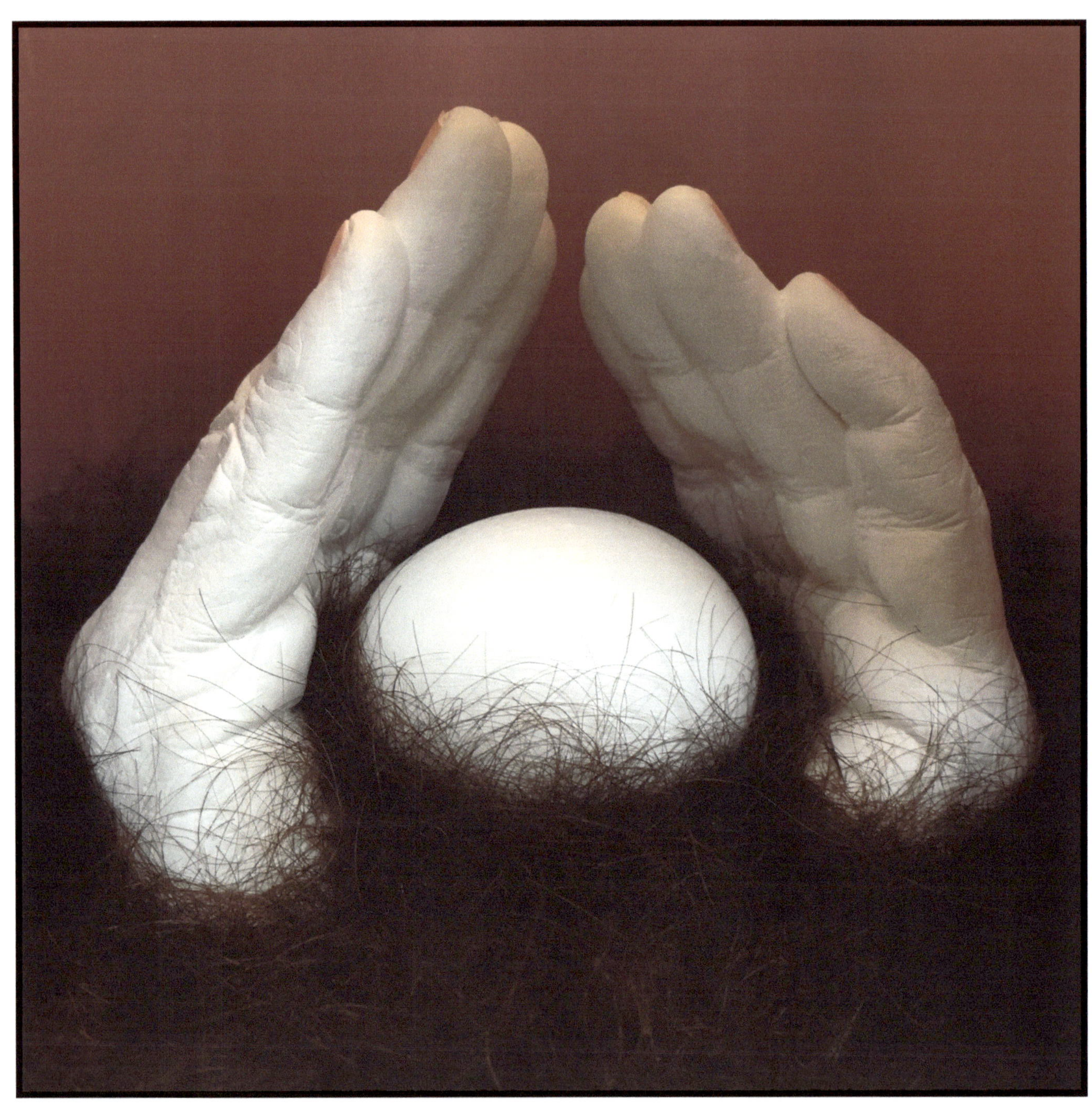

(Inside View)

About "PLEASED TO MEET YOU"

I began and now am. My first self-portrait, if made to scale, would have been much less than 12" x 12" x 12". In pondering my "No Big Heads" sculpture that was accepted in the 2022 "No Big Heads" national art competition (University of Alaska Anchorage), I thought of my mother and my first journey with her, in her, and how surprised and delighted we must have been when we finally met.

Materials:

Artist's hair, acrylic painted plaster mold of artist's hands, acrylic painted hollow chicken egg, altered and hand painted baby dress, custom fabricated pink cloth, altered lampshade painted with acrylic inside and out, ribbon, wood base.

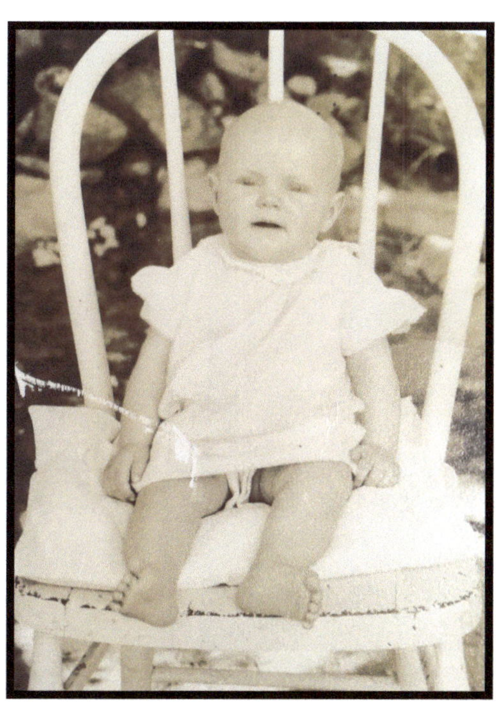

My mother as a baby

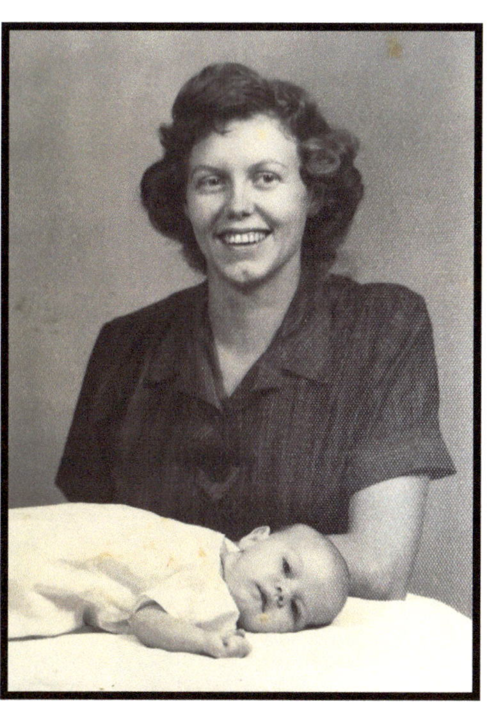

Mom and me

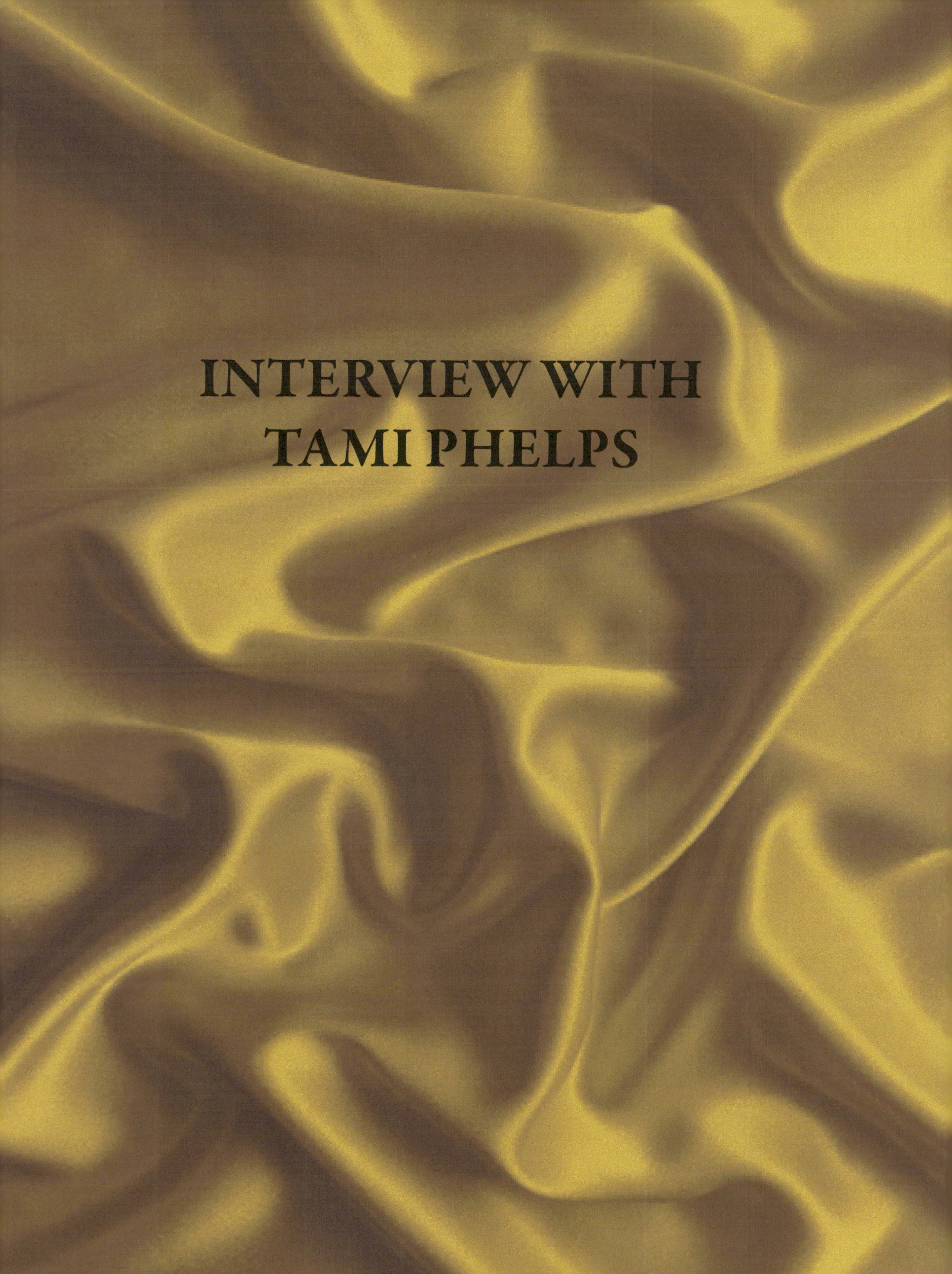

INTERVIEW WITH
TAMI PHELPS

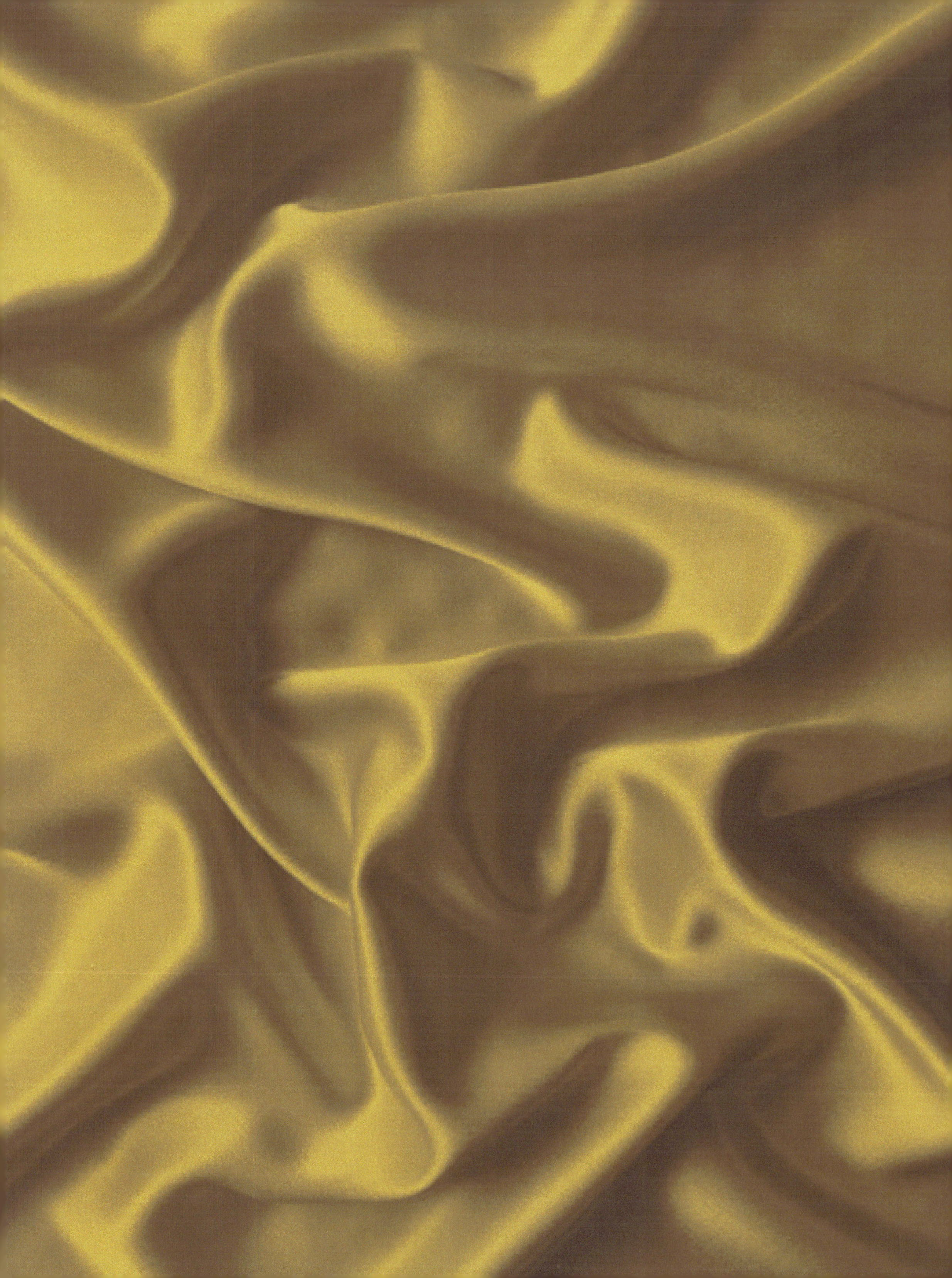

Interview with Tami Phelps about her 14 art pieces in *The Woman Within* and life as an artist. October 13, 2022. In her living room, surrounded by the art works hanging on the wall.

Interview by Kerry Dean Feldman.

Kerry Dean Feldman: Would you tell me what got you started on this collection of work?

Tami Phelps: Absolutely. This first one is called "Meet Willow," and it was the first one I painted with the little dress on it. This started the whole idea of painting on my substrate in a way that camouflaged the dress, but yet told a story. This was a story of a little girl in Alaska lying or hiding in the willow trees, maybe birch trees, kind of playing in nature.

The next one here—and there in no particular order except how I see them on the wall right now—the next one is "Her Metamorphosis." This one is probably the most detailed story that I've painted. This one takes me back to when I was probably four years old in Sidney, Nebraska. In our back yard there was a water pump. It was a very hot day, and I was standing by the water pump. All of a sudden all of these monarch butterflies came and landed on me. It was magical, just magical. I thought it was because they just loved me. So, I stood there like a statue. It turns out they were thirsty—and I was at a water pump, but I still remember it to this day. Inside the little dress I put a hand embroidered uterus. It's in a bag that is open, with butterflies flying out of it. The butterflies have metamorphosed as will the little girl.

The next one I see I call "Meet Aurora." It is so happy and cheerful, and the colors I chose for this are like the northern lights or the aurora borealis. I like the movement in this painting.

Another one I see is called "Meet Zinnia." (My friend, Laura, helped me name this painting.) For this one, rather than a portrait orientation, I've turned it to be more of a landscape which was a very different feel. It allowed me to spread the dress out in a different way. I wanted to try a different technique, so with the flowers I tied coins in them with a string and stabilized them with a starch. I took the strings off them, removed the coins, and circles of fabric formed in the center of these little flowers. Zinnia flowers. It's a texture difference that is not found on the other paintings. I was very pleased with this new technique. It added depth.

Another one here I call, "One Size Does Not Fit All." This in a way is kind of a nod to mom. She had my big sister Sue and me take sewing lessons. At the time we really didn't want to, but I am so glad she did. Throughout the art that I have made over the years, I have altered and sewn lots of fabric. On this one I have altered the pattern.

The next one I see is called, "Grounded in Winter." This piece has a dress on it that I have printed on with a previous cold wax painting using tissue paper. It's a bare tree, and kind of a stark blue color so it just feels very winter-like to me. One of the things that I added to it, on the background behind the little dress, is a series of leaves, dried leaves, that I've collected, pressed, adhered, and painted over, so there's a very textural background. It is in the winter with the leaves kind of camouflaged.

This one I call, "Meet Flora." For this piece, I painted the background with some of the roots growing off of the dress into the ground below. The flowers are made of some lace that I had. I extended them with some strings, thick for the stems. All of my dresses are painted with cold wax and oil medium, with some acrylic as well. "Meet Flora" is very textural, grounded with the roots on the bottom. (My friend, Vickie, suggested this title.)

The next one I call, "Meet Daisy." This one was sheer joy. I just love the little girl dress and daisy flowers with the free hand painting of the daisies. I used the lines in the dress as stems that were textured and bunched up when I adhered the dress. It makes me happy. I do love this sweet little girl.

The painting beneath it on the wall is called, "The Day It Started." This one started out completely different than how it turned out, which is the case for much of my art. I really like the movement, depth, patterns, and the sculptural quality of this piece. The shapes feel very organic to me. Across the middle of this little girl's dress is kind of a belt and all of the little dots or periods, if you will, are white. The last one has a little spot of red on it. It indicates the day she started her period. There's an innocence to it, yet the dress style indicates a bit more of a mature girl than, say, the daisy dress. This one is called "The Day It Started." And I do remember the day it started; most girls probably do.

The painting next to it is called, "Expectations." This one has a lot of meaning to me. It has to do with the expectations of oneself, what you think you'll be when you grow up or what you think will happen when you grow up and also the expectations of others. The inside of the dress is being held open with little hands revealing a nest. One of the things that I always thought would happen was that I would have children, but I didn't. It's expected by society, I believe, that women have children. People assume you have them and when you don't it's... I don't know... it's noticeable to me. It's never mentioned in a harsh way, but I do think about it. So, this is called, "Expectations." It kind of makes me sad, to tell you the truth, but it's cathartic to make art about it. A lot of art that I do has to do with having babies or not having babies.

This next one I call, "Meet Melody." Just the structure of this dress really looked musical to me. The lines and the ruffles at the bottom have kind of a musical staff feeling to them. I have incorporated a collage of musical notes on the bottom that are kind of hidden and moving and dancing around in the dress. I also have some lupine or wildflowers of sorts that are in the dress. Since my dad is a musician, I have a lot of art that incorporates music. This one just makes me happy. Many of my dress paintings have elements of nature in them, including this one. And I love the colors in this piece.

The one hanging above it I call "The Autumn of her Life." The intent with this one is that I have painted the dress to be a little worn, a little faded in color. The middle of the dress with the opening with the leaf…it's a dry leaf…represents an older woman. The time for youth has passed. She's moving on to her autumn years. In the background of this piece are tissue prints from paintings I have done previously with the color palette that I thought was autumn-like. I like the pattern of this melancholy piece.

"Meet Rose" is the next painting. The details on this dress are very intricate, and Victorian-looking to me. I painted this with some of my favorite colors. I truly love the combination of the peach and marigold-ish colors. Included on the frilly hem are tiny dry rose petals I collected over the years. It just looks very feminine to me. I think there are a lot of stories this little girl could tell.

The final one I have here is kind of a timely piece with a nod to Ruth Bader Ginsburg. The lace collar around it tells the story, an iconic symbol of Ruth Bader Ginsburg. The dress itself is a dark black dress on the blue background, with kind of a golden glow, kind of a halo effect around the top. I painted this on the occasion of her death.

All these paintings started off with an antique vintage white dress. I painted them in a way that has the movement I was looking for, with the suggestion of different stories that I had in mind. Some of the stories I knew, some of them evolved, some of the pieces are experimentations with different techniques. All of them are filled with meaning. I love to go to antique stores, look at things, and imagine the lives lived with the items, the stories they might tell. That's what I tried to do with these dresses. This is the backstory on "The Woman Within" collection.

KDF: Did you find all these vintage dresses yourself at stores?

TP: No, I didn't. Over the time, some friends have known I paint with vintage dresses and have given dresses to me to work with. This is such a gift because their personal stories are also in them. I made a sculpture with one dress that a friend of mine actually wore as a child. She said to do whatever I wanted with it. It turned out to be the sculpture featured in this book—"Pleased To Meet You." When I showed it to her, she said she had no idea that it would become that. Neither did I.

KDF: Did you paint these during the winter, summer, fall, or is there any seasonal influence? What's going on outside of you while you're painting these.

TP: Well, the first one I did, as I mentioned, was "Meet Willow," and that one was probably in the fall a couple of years ago.

KDF: Was it during the first COVID fall?

TP: No, it was before COVID. I had been invited to do a solo exhibit with these dresses, then COVID hit, and it had to be cancelled. But I kept painting. I had the need to complete this collection. So, I have.

KDF: How do you attach these dresses to the wood substrate?

TP: Since I paint with cold wax and oil, I have to really think backwards because glue or any kind of adhesion won't last, won't be archival on top of wax. The cradle board substrate that I use is prepared with gesso. On that I often paint with acrylic, then I paint over the acrylic with gel medium that is an artist quality glue, if you will. Then I'm able to adhere the actual fabric to the board. I just slather underneath and on top of the fabric with gel medium that allows me to kind of "sculpt" the fabric. When that dries, then I am able to apply the cold wax and oil which will adhere to that. So, there are a lot of stages that I have to think about with the layers that I do, knowing that I can only paint on top of the dried gel medium with cold wax and oil.

KDF: How long might it take a layer to do one of these? Like "Meet Rose." Like, a day, two days?

TP: It takes a long time. Let's see … I often have a couple pieces in the works because of the drying time. Cold wax takes a long time to dry. If I had a finished piece with all the stages that I do…there's probably three or four difference time periods that I spend on a dress. And each time period takes a day to three or four days to dry, so I have to work on something in between. It takes a good long time for me to do one, probably a week. But on top of that, to really cure and dry takes another week or longer. Cold wax cures through evaporation and time.

KDF: So. you have fourteen pieces in this collection. And it might take two weeks each, so about twenty-eight weeks. That would be about seven months.

TP: I've never really thought of it that way, but, yes, it's quite a long time. I do have another one that didn't make the grade, but it was a really good learning experience for me, and I could possibly refine it. I don't know that I'm finished with this idea. I keep going back to femininity and stories about "she-ness" which is evident in the other work that I've done. I have more dresses that I've collected so I could certainly do more. Maybe I will someday. But this feels done for now.

KDF: In terms of the challenge of doing this how does this work on femininity of "The Woman Within" compare, to let us say, "Her Stories" in which there are only eight, and they're very personal, each of them, for you in terms of just you as an artist.

Are they more complex or less complex or different or did you grow, or is it just the same thing or what?

TP: It's not the same thing. It's very different as far as techniques; it's also very different as far as the stories that each of them tells. These little dresses that I've done, "The Woman Within" dresses, are kind of a universal story about a woman within a child and it's more diverse as far as the cultural aspects. The woman within each girl is not necessarily me. Some of them could be, but they contain more universal stories. With the attachment of the dresses on my substrate in "The Woman Within," it's mostly fabric adhered to my substrate. With the other collection, "Her Stories," I have added a lot of assemblage, a lot of other items to them. The main thing being metal "scrolls" used to tell their stories. As I mentioned earlier, with cold wax it's not archival if you just glue items on the wax. It won't stick and stay. I really had to think about what I was going to adhere to tell the story, and how I was going to do it with "Her Stories." I had to think backwards from the finished product. How do I attach this, how do I attach that? A layered way of thinking from the finished product back to the beginning. For example, on the "Her Do-Over' Recital" I've got the piano keys attached to the metal scroll. The scroll is attached with wire on top of the painting that I did. Each of them has more ephemera attached to them than the dresses. I had to think about how to adhere all the items. They are more sculptural paintings than the dresses. "Her Stories" have more personal stories than "The Woman Within." They are mostly stories about me and my family as I was growing up as a kid, about my dad, mom, brothers and sister, and some people I know in my life. So, the dress collection is more universal than my assemblage paintings. But they are similar in that they're both about children and women in particular.

KDF: So, "The Woman Within" collection is more universal. When you painted "One Size Does Not Fit All," using all the patterns, did you have any notion of the diversity in womanhood or is it just honoring your mother? Did you have in mind the diversity of womanhood when you started this work, or did it evolve?

TP: A lot of times when you go shopping, you'll see a tag that says, "One size fits all." Well, that's not true. Women are not all the same size. That made me think that not all women started out the same or all end the same. Sometimes there are changes in peoples' lives and sometimes people who are female feel like a male, and vice-versa. It's just assumed that when you see a woman, she's always been a woman. That does not fit all. People make changes and personal choices in their life. So, this piece has to do with not just the size but also the other changes people make.

KDF: You were a teacher before your career as an artist. You also taught art in your Montessori classroom in Anchorage. Did you learn about diversity through interacting with your students? A lot of them keep in touch with you for ten or twenty years or more. Did you learn from your students about the diversity of girls?

TP: Oh sure, sure! I have learned a lot from the kids about the diversity of how they looked at themselves then and how they look at themselves now. And some of the kids that I've known in school (not necessarily in my classroom) have had a gender change. They are not what they used to be, or what other people assumed they were. They're different now, and happier. A little bit more...what?...true to themselves. So, one size certainly does not fit all.

KDF: OK. Thanks. And maybe a final question. In your experience of womanhood and girlhood, do men influence that in a positive way or a negative way? Or is it only women... and maybe you haven't thought about this... how did that dialogue occur? I mean, did you have to outgrow certain self-images? Did men help you? Do women sometimes put lids on themselves?

TP: A lot to think about. Yes, I've thought about it. Both men and women put lids on people. It's not just men or just women. There are a lot of influences that I have thought about with these pieces. I think I keep going back to my parents and I know that my dad had a huge influence on me and the rest of us kids with his musical background. I find that a very positive thing and something that I'm able to draw on. And with mom…we didn't really have a great deal of money and mom was always very creative with the things that we did have. She could make things and art out of very little; she was very resourceful. I like to think out of the box as a result. That just feels right. I think we all have to outgrow different feelings and different restrictions from both men and woman. Making art is kind of a way for me to do that. I'd have to think more about it before I give you a clear answer. I'm not really sure if I answered what you asked.

KDF: You did. Thanks. In the introduction to this book, you quote "a former gymnastics coach." So…some of these might appear to be kind of girly-girl art pieces, but in your own life there was a lot of athleticism and activity. You were the pogo-stick champion of your block, someplace. So, what was that about, being a pogo-stick champion, and a girl? I mean, did you feel competitive? Who got the pogo-stick?

TP: Yes (laughing), I felt competitive, and I loved that pogo-stick. It was kind of a thing where I jumped on it so much that in the morning when I woke up, I still felt like I was jumping.

KDF: How old were you?

TP: I must have been second or third grade. I just loved it. And then rope swings. Oh, gosh, dad made rope swings for us in every back yard where we lived over the years, and one of them was in our living room. I write about it in the book, in "Her Dad's Metronome." I was just enthralled with rope swings, and I knew that I was going to run away and join the circus and be a "type-rope walker" (both laugh).

KDF: Your youngest brother played in the circus, didn't he?

TP: (Laughing) Yes, my youngest brother, Jim, played drums in the circus.

KDF: And he has a degree in music. He's an incredible musician. So, what got you interested in gymnastics? I mean, a person can get hurt… I would never do gymnastics.

TP: Well, again, mom signed my sister Sue and I up for lessons. This time it was in Mary Funk's school of dance. We took tap dance. I really loved it. (Laughing). I recently found out my sister didn't and I always thought she did. I did a lot of things; tap dancing and gymnastics, pogo-sticks and rope swings. My favorite was the balance beam (in gymnastics). I was very athletic, very competitive, but also really enjoyed the physicality of doing things. It wasn't just the guys who could do it, although when I first started gymnastics in seventh grade, we had to wait until the boys were finished with their basketball and wrestling. We had to go in after them in a stinky old little room with all the sweaty mats. It was clear that girls were definitely thought of as second-class citizens. I've got a lot of memories about that over the years. Thankfully that has changed. Mrs. Shaw was my gymnastics coach. Oh, she was very, very strict and very gymnastics-coach-like. I really admired her. She taught me a lot and it wasn't just about gymnastics.

KDF: So, I understand that you competed in "All-Around" gymnastics competition in high school in Anchorage. You were in West High, an Eagle.

TP: Yes. I really loved balance beam. That was my best event. Floor exercise I really liked. Vaulting was tricky and the uneven bars I avoided at all costs. Mrs. Shaw made me do all four of them in one meet as an "All-Around" competitor. We were competing against the East High Thunderbirds. There was a girl on the East High team named Tammy N. And, my name, being Tami also, we listened for the announcements of who won, and what the highest score was at the end of the meet. I had done particularly well on the beam and was sure I won. Then they announced *the first-place winner of the balance beam is... Tammyyyyy...N.* It wasn't me, so I did not get a first place. I don't really remember what I did get. I think I did place, but I was never the best. I always tried, and I truly loved it.

KDF: OK. Thank you. I've noticed there's a lot of hammering and sawing and cutting and drilling and making of things besides this painting in your art loft. Is that something that runs in your family or is that just you?

TP: Hm, I'd have to say it runs in the family. I know when we first moved up here in 1970, dad, mom, and us kids basically dug the foundation for an add-on to the house. And dad, a professional musician, actually built the house. He knew how to do all of that; I knew that he could make rope swings and tree forts out of piano crates. We had some great tree forts, tree houses. And mom could make something out of nothing, so, creativity runs in the family. I have three younger brothers and I have to say that they are extremely creative and resourceful. They have a lot of ideas of ways to make things. My brother, Jay, made an "Ordinary," a tall two-wheel 1880s bicycle, maybe five feet high, with a seat in the middle. You had to stand on a ladder to get on it. He made this out of different parts. The trick was finding a fence to hang on to when you needed to stop. Jay is always making something. He looks at things and creates different ways to use them. It's amazing. He'll send me things to use for my art. I'll mention something and he'll send a rusty piece of metal that might be good for this or that. My brothers Jay and Jim worked together on a boat in Hawaii. This boat was in major need of repair—a thirty-six foot boat that they patched and built and rebuilt. Who knew that they knew how to do that? My brother, John, made a toboggan out of straight wood. He was able to steam it, bend it, so he had a toboggan. He makes incredible furniture, redid his fireplace. I've called on him more than once to help me with measuring and cutting something that I needed. I do a lot of pounding and cutting but I don't have my own workshop, so I do go to John. He made a table for me, for my loft, out of a door, an antique door that I had. And made me a metal steel desk that we had to lift over the outdoor balcony, then up and over the loft ledge. I mean, they're not afraid to do anything. I get that from mom and dad; my brothers do, too. My sister is also extremely creative. She does felting, stained glass, and makes jewelry. If you need canning, she and her husband grow veggies and fruit and make jelly and jam and can their own everything. She and I, as I mentioned, danced together and we've been a duo ever since. There is a piece that I have that features my sister and it's in the *Amaryllis* collection. It's called "Shadowing." There's a picture, probably my most favorite picture of my sister and me, that I use in that piece. I have shadowed my sister, Sue, for many years and she taught me so many things, not intentionally, not directly, but I have learned from her. I have learned from all my family. Creativity definitely runs in the family.

Oh, there was one other thing I wanted to say. With these scrolls that I have on "Her Stories," my brothers Jim and Jay, and I, went to a recycled hardware store in Portland. I found a bucket of metal rods. I really didn't know what they were. I knew I could probably use them. For something. And, sure enough, I have used them. My brother, Jay, taught me how to rust them up. Through him I got a start on how to make them more rusty. Jim took me to that place because he knew how much I liked to treasure hunt. I wanted to mention that; another example of how my brothers have helped me.

KDF: I think I recall a box that was shipped here or did we bring it with us? How'd we get that box here?

TP: Oh, that's a box of other stuff, a box of some metal that I bought and have yet to use. I'll make something out of them. They are metal printer plates. They're a little larger than an eight by ten sheet of paper. They were used back in the day, I think, to set type on them. Printers used individual letters and set up a type—they'd put them on these metal trays. I will use them. I haven't yet, but they were a really good price (laughs). So, that's what we shipped here.

KDF: If you had a barn, which it seems to me you need, what would you do? What kind of art would you do? If you had a barn?

TP: I would make it a really cool art studio, with a workshop with all of the tools I need, including table saws and miters. I'm really drawn to making furniture, as well. I print my art on fabric and reupholster furniture. Right now, I have to go with furniture that I find in antique stores, which is fine, I love doing that, but at some point, I'd love to make my own furniture and frames. I would also have a painting studio with great light. I would also have, well, just space to create.

KDF: So, that's "feminine"?

TP: Sure. It is. I can do it. I love it. I'd love to be an inspiration to others.

KDF: Thank you, Tami. I hope folks enjoy learning how Tami conceived of and made this art.

TAMI PHELPS: ARTIST STATEMENT

As a former Montessori teacher, many of the concepts I use in my artwork are rooted in the pedagogical philosophy of the Italian educator, anthropologist, physician, scientist, and promoter of education for peace, Dr. Maria Montessori. An example is my reference to nature (air, land, and water) in many of my paintings. I like to tell stories through my art. On the pages of *The Woman Within* are photographs of examples of my visual storytelling about "she-ness" over the past ten years.

I have shifted my focus as a visual artist from hand-colored photography to primarily painting with cold wax medium. My photographs are sometimes included in my artwork, as are other assemblages, often including vintage items. I rarely pass up an antique store where I can get lost in my thoughts about lives lived through the treasures I find, and the "what if" possibilities I see in them. Music, nature, and family are also elements that inspire and shape my paintings. Conceptual paintings about global warming have become a recent focus for my storytelling through visual art. I like to offer paintings that make people, including myself, think, wonder, question, and appreciate beauty, sometimes in unexpected ways.

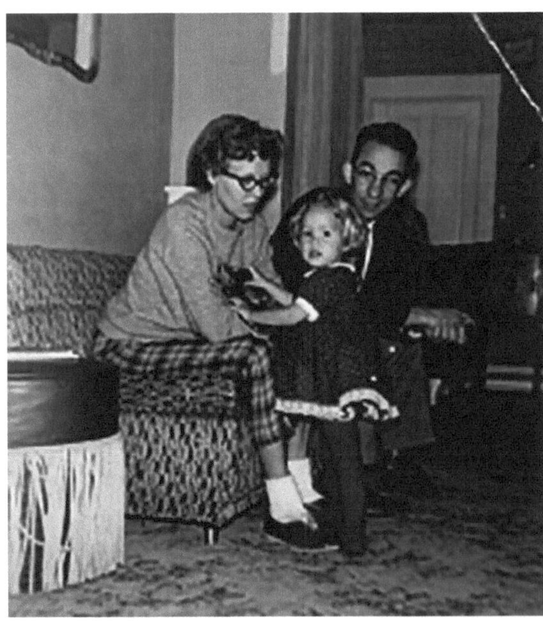

Me with my mother and father, Ardis and Sid Phelps.

BIO

After packing five kids and all of our belongings in one car and one truck, mom and dad drove us north to Alaska on the Alcan Highway from "the Lower 48" in 1970. Anchorage has been my home since then. I attended college and Montessori education in Hawaii, Arizona, Colorado, and Washington, receiving my B.Ed. degree from University of Alaska Anchorage. I studied cold wax medium painting under several local and nationally prominent artists. I often tell stories through my conceptual paintings and have shared these through solo and group exhibits in Alaska, Washington, South Dakota, Colorado, Arizona, New Mexico, and Rhode Island as well as in international competitions. My artwork is included in the permanent collections of the Anchorage Museum in Alaska, and the Museum of Encaustic Art, Santa Fe, New Mexico. It is also in numerous private collections in Alaska and the Lower 48. Notable publications that include my paintings are *Cirque* (cirquejournal. com), *Vignettes in Wax and Words* (international-encaustic-artists.org), and *50 States/50 Artists* (eainm.com). My art is on the cover of *Drunk on Love: Twelve Stories to Savor Responsibly* (Cirque Press, 2019, by Kerry Dean Feldman), and twice on the covers of *Cirque: A Literary Journal for the North Pacific Rim* (Vol.8, No.2 and Vol.12, No.1). I am co-author with Kerry Dean Feldman of *Miss Tami Is Today Tomorrow? Kindergarten in Alaska: Stories for Grown-Ups* (Cirque Press, 2021), illustrated by Tammy Murray. I am a four-time invited Artist-In-Resident at McKinley Chalet Lodge, Denali National Park, Alaska. tamiphelps.com

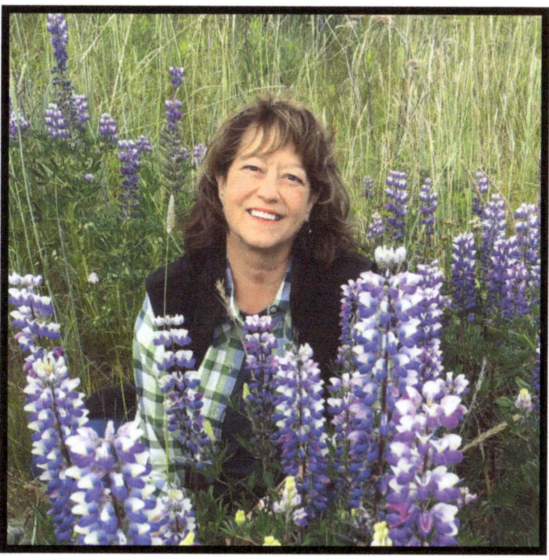

Tami Phelps
Photograph by Kerry Dean Feldman

KERRY DEAN FELDMAN: ARTIST STATEMENT

I watched Tami create and grapple with these art works over a COVID winter in Anchorage. I responded to her questions about them. After they were done, and their initial exhibition was canceled in Anchorage due to COVID, I suggested I write poems related to them, about my awareness as a man of the woman within a girl. Maybe we do a book, an exhibition. She liked the idea and gave me no limits in what I might write.

To me, we invent each other—we women and men—but within cultural worlds that we do not invent—and they change; cultures always change. This change can be threatening to anyone in the tens of thousands of cultural imaginations about the meaning of life that erupted on earth. Why? Because each culture proclaims it has absolute truth, forever, including *what's a woman, a man,* and prescribes the proper roles and behaviors and attire for each—and the taboos for being accepted as a man or woman.

Women influenced my life, formed me, as much as the macho Western man myths of my Montana youth (which I loved). Women helped free me from many stereotypes about gender (am still learning), beginning with my mother who was very feminine, but she taught me how to fight with my fists when a bigger neighbor boy threatened me if my dog pooped in his yard.

Gender in any culture is like a braided rope, one strand here, another there, intertwining to form a bond of meaning, partly based on our biology, partly invented. For example, a woman could not put her name on a work of art in Europe until the second half of the 19th century. That is, *ALL or a lot of Western civilization* until the end of the 19th century into the 20th century has a loony and extremely harmful androcentric basis for both boys and girls. It dies only slowly and is still vibrant in much of Europe and the US (almost worldwide). It's a cultural invention, based on the perceived inferior biology of woman. Women actually have two copies of the X chromosome on which most (over 90%) of our genes as humans reside. It makes just as much sense to say *only women can paint and sculpt which is their God-given right as superior beings* and men should put a sister's name on his art.

My poems reflect my growing awareness of *The Woman Within* a girl.

BIO

Kerry Dean Feldman has called Alaska home since 1973. He was born and raised in rural eastern Montana to homesteader and railroad ancestors. He's currently a professor emeritus in anthropology at the University of Alaska Anchorage after a four-decade career (PhD, University of Colorado, Boulder). Five Star/Gale (Maine) published his historical western novel, *Alice's Trading Post: A Novel of the West* (2022). Cirque Press published several poems in *Cirque* journal, his short story collection, *Drunk on Love; Twelve Stories to Savor Responsibly* (2019), and his noir murder mystery set in Montana, *Kettle Dance: Murder in the Big Sky* (2022). The *Terry Tribune* (Montana) published his first poem when he was seven, "The Owl," about a hoot owl in his family's barn. He lives in Anchorage, Alaska with his wife, artist Tami Phelps.

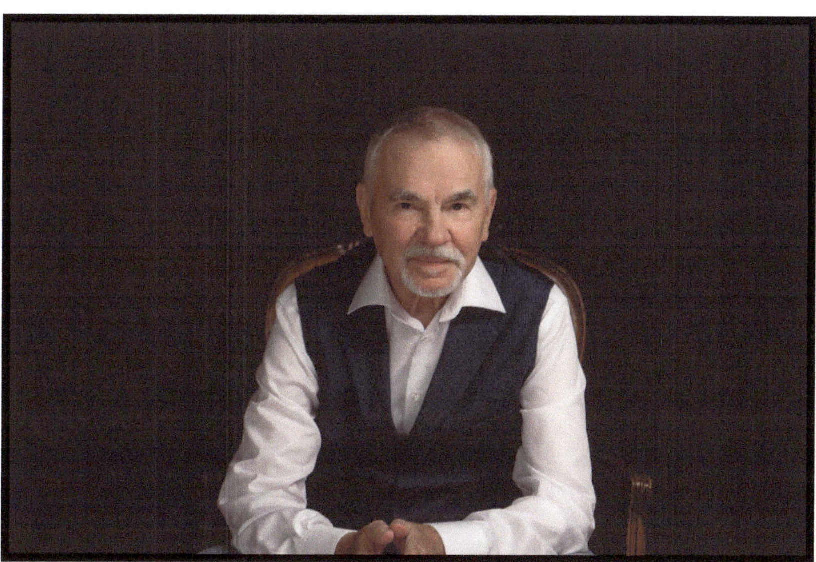

Kerry Feldman
Photograph by Dori Yelverton

RICHARD J. MURPHY: ARTIST STATEMENT

The project of photographing a single amaryllis plant through its life cycle is part of a photographic meditation on life, death, and loss that began with the photographic documentation of my wife Bonnie Bernholz's battle with, and death from, breast cancer.

The parallels between a human life and that of a flower seemed an obvious path, from the emergence of a sprout, to the voluminous beauty of full bloom, through the decline of age, to the dry fragility of death. Using a variety of cameras and techniques, it was a daily exercise of investigating form, texture, light, and the feelings evoked as the plant grew, faded and died. Some blossoms were pressed and dried in the traditional manner, some were allowed to air dry in sculptural forms to be rephotographed.

When the project was officially completed, it felt very incomplete. I took dozens of prints and some dried flowers to my friend, the polymath artist Tami Phelps, whose work I have admired for many years. Although she knew both my wife and my work, we recognized that she could take the images and make them her own, telling her own story through them. I was overjoyed when she accepted this admittedly strange challenge. But I could never have imagined the complex and wonderful tale she would weave with those photographs. Tami took the work in a completely different direction from my original narrative, and she built a story of love, connection and femininity infused with depth and compassion.

I'm not sure I could work like this with another artist. I have such respect for Tami and her work that I felt my images were in good hands. But even with that trust and faith, I had no idea what a wonderful series would come of our collaboration, *Growing Panes:Reflections on an Amaryllis.*

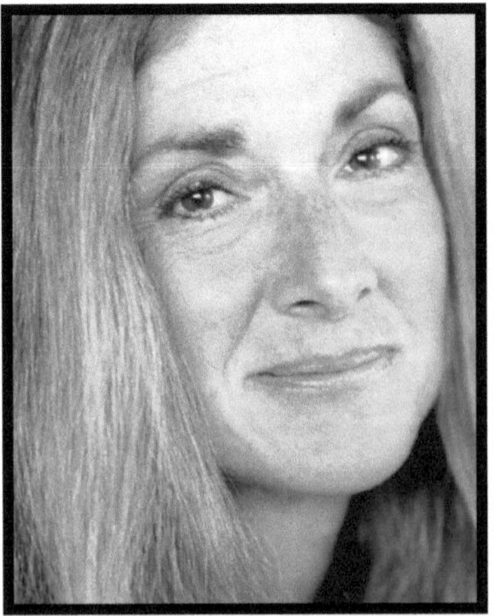

Bonnie Bernholz
Photograph by Richard J. Murphy

BIO

Richard J. Murphy spent his professional career as a newspaper photojournalist. He was the chief photographer of the *Jackson Hole News* (Wyoming) for ten years before serving 25 years as photo editor of the *Anchorage Daily News* (Alaska). He has been the Atwood Chair of Journalism at the University of Alaska Anchorage, and the Snedden Chair of Journalism at the University of Alaska Fairbanks. During his time as a photojournalist, Murphy also pursued his personal photographic work, primarily images of nature. His current work addresses the effects of climate change in the natural world.

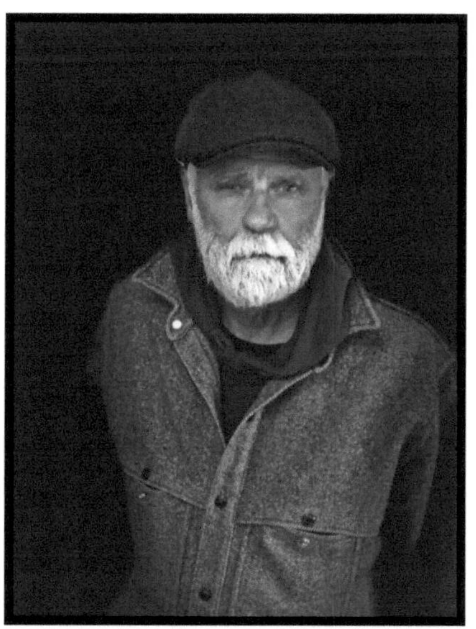

Richard J. Murphy
Photograph by Will Murphy

ABOUT CIRQUE PRESS

Cirque Press grew out of Cirque, a literary journal that publishes the works of writers and artists from the North Pacific Rim, a region that reaches north from Oregon to the Yukon Territory, south through Alaska to Hawaii, and west to the Russian Far East.

Cirque Press is a partnership of Sandra Kleven, publisher, and Michael Burwell, editor. Ten years ago, we recognized that works of talented writers in the region were going unpublished, and the Press was launched to bring those works to fruition. We publish fiction, nonfiction, and poetry, and we seek to produce art that provides a deeper understanding about the region and its cultures. The writing of our authors is significant, personal, and strong.

Sandra Kleven – Michael Burwell, publishers and editors

www.cirquejournal.com

BOOKS FROM CIRQUE PRESS

Apportioning the Light by Karen Tschannen (2018)

The Lure of Impermanence by Carey Taylor (2018)

Echolocation by Kristin Berger (2018)

Like Painted Kites & Collected Works by Clifton Bates (2019)

Athabaskan Fractal: Poems of the Far North by Karla Linn Merrifield (2019)

Holy Ghost Town by Tim Sherry (2019)

Drunk on Love: Twelve Stories to Savor Responsibly by Kerry Dean Feldman (2019)

Wide Open Eyes: Surfacing from Vietnam by Paul Kirk Haeder (2020)

Silty Water People by Vivian Faith Prescott (2020)

Life Revised by Leah Stenson (2020)

Oasis Earth: Planet in Peril by Rick Steiner (2020)

The Way to Gaamaak Cove by Doug Pope (2020)

Loggers Don't Make Love by Dave Rowan (2020)

The Dream That Is Childhood by Sandra Wassilie (2020)

Seward Soundboard by Sean Ulman (2020)

The Fox Boy by Gretchen Brinck (2021)

Lily Is Leaving: Poems by Leslie Ann Fried (2021)

One Headlight by Matt Caprioli (2021)

November Reconsidered by Marc Janssen (2021)

Someday I'll Miss This Place Too by Dan Branch (2021)

Out There In The Out There by Jerry McDonnell (2021)

Fish the Deep Water Hard by Eric Heyne (2021)

Salt & Roses by Buffy McKay (2022)

Growing Older In This Place: A Life in Alaska's Rainforest by Margo Wasserman Waring (2022)

Kettle Dance: A Big Sky Murder by Kerry Dean Feldman (2022)

Nothing Got Broke by Larry F. Slonaker (2022)

Sky Changes on the Kuskokwim by Clifton Bates (2022)

Transplanted: A Memoir by Birgit Sarrimanolis (2022)

Between Promise and Sadness by Joanne Townsend (2022)

Yosemite Dawning by Shauna Potocky (2022)

CIRCLES

Illustrated books from Cirque Press

Baby Abe: A Lullaby for Lincoln – Ann Chandonnet (2021)

Miss Tami, Is Today Tomorrow? – Tami Phelps (2021)

Miss Bebe Goes to America by Lynda Humphrey (2022)

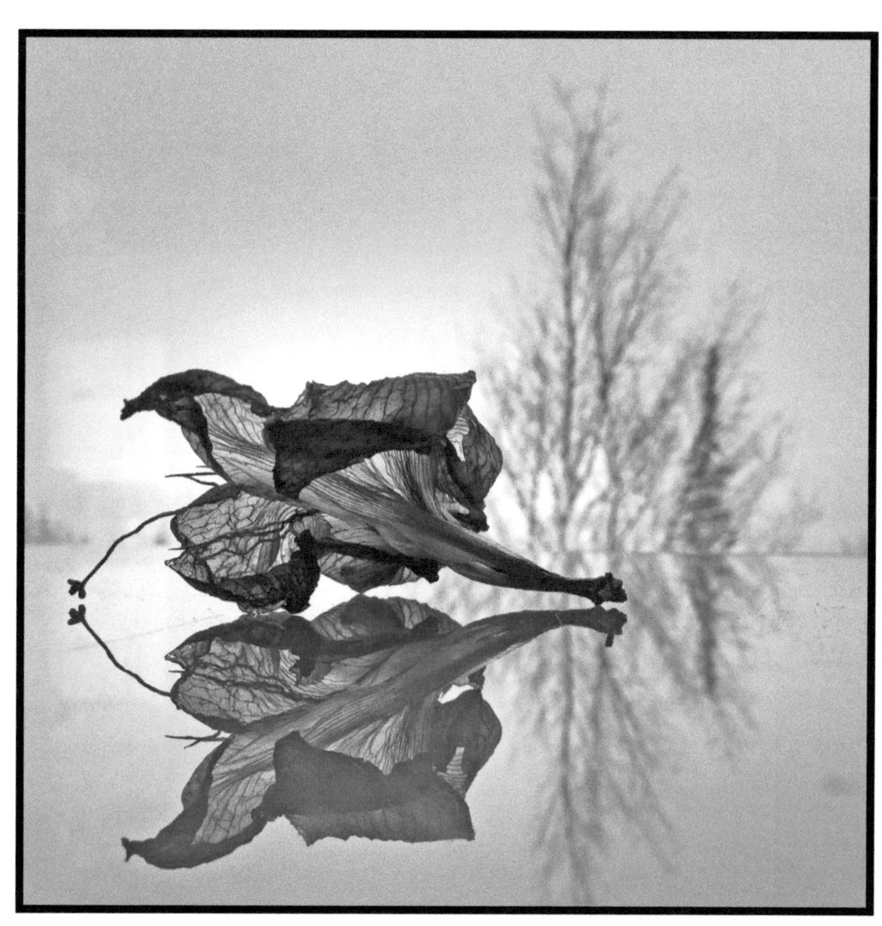

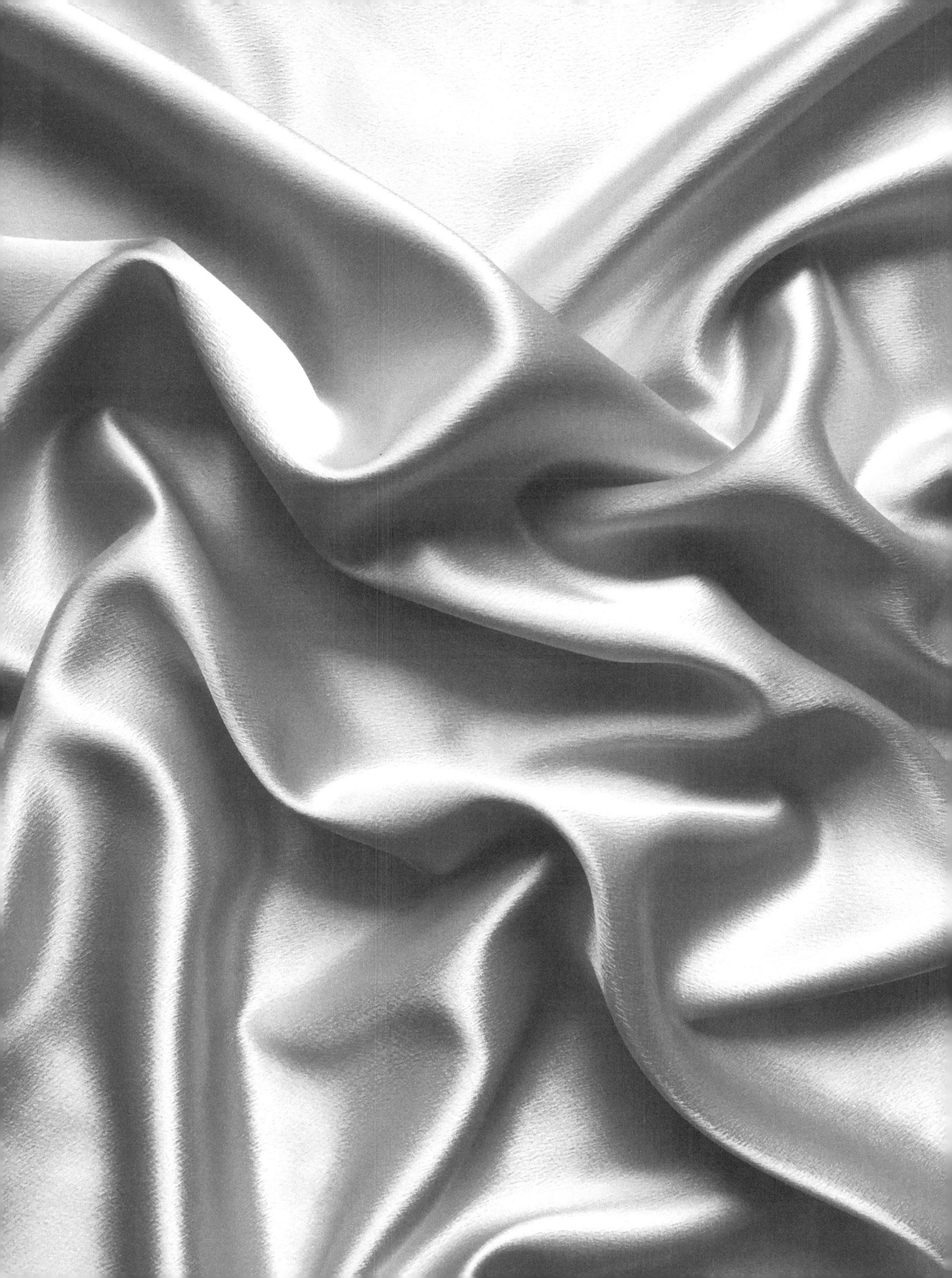

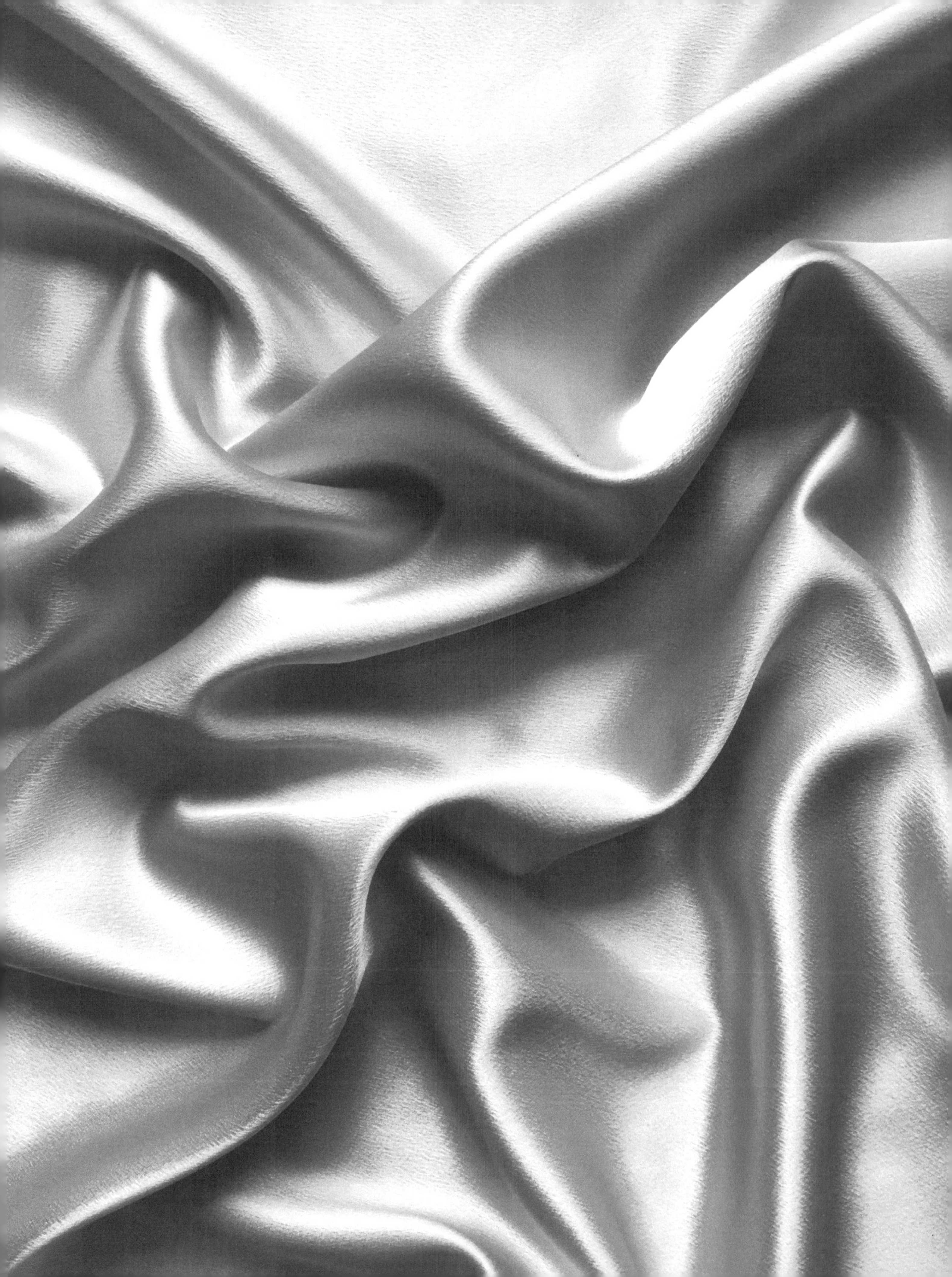

www.ingramcontent.com/pod-product-compliance
Lightning Source LLC
Chambersburg PA
CBHW041641110726
48005CB00003B/667